The Holy Spirit...
Heaven's Sherpa

JACQUELINE PEART

The Holy Spirit… Heaven's Sherpa

Copyright © October 2023 by Jacqueline Peart

Printed in the United Kingdom

Editorial and Design Production: The Editor's Chair

International Standard Book Number: 978-1-907137-11-2

In loving memory of my dad,
Ivan Harold Peart

~~~

Contents

SECTION FOUR
The Holy Spirit... Heaven's Sherpa

SECTION FIVE
Cultivating Your Relationship with the Holy Spirit

FURTHER INFORMATION

Dedication

Holy Spirit, Heaven's Sherpa, this book is Yours. Without You, the words within would lack the transformative power to inspire, heal or deliver. So, I pray that as each person reads this book, they will encounter you in ways they have never done so before. I pray they cooperate with you, allowing you to be the Guide and Counsellor Jesus said you would be, in Jesus' name.

To every person reading this book who is ready to embark on the next level of their journey with God, I dedicate the writing of this book to you. As I write, I am praying for you. I am also shedding tears of hope. I believe that you will encounter the Holy Spirit in ways you have only heard or read about—until now, in Jesus' name.

To my handpicked, called and deeply-loved family (Peart, Atkinson and JPIM), everything I do for His glory has been backed up by your support and championship. I pray you, too, experience the Holy Spirit in your lives in a way you have never done before or even thought possible, in Jesus' name. The best is yet to come!

Disclaimer

The Holy Spirit… Heaven's Sherpa comes with a disclaimer. The contents of this book have not been written for, or from, an academic or theological perspective, though my theology will be evident throughout. I recognise there is a cross-section of beliefs, doctrine, and theological perspectives on the Holy Spirit—ranging from the doctrine of cessationism that teaches speaking in tongues, prophecy and healing, for example, ceased after Jesus' ascension, to teachings that they remain fully operational on Earth today, evidenced by the power, gifts and attributes of the Holy Spirit.

Wherever you sit along this spectrum, please read with an open heart. Allow the Holy Spirit, Heaven's Sherpa, to guide you to new heights and depths in Him, in Jesus' name.

Foreword

I t has been our great joy and pleasure to have known Apostle Jacqueline Peart for over a decade. She is an excellent communicator and an exceptional writer of poetry and devotional material. She has a style all of her own borne out of her incredible creative ability and her unique apostolic anointing. The two together are a powerful force! My wife and I have studied the subject of the Holy Spirit and taught it over the past 36 years of full-time pastoral ministry. This book was like a fresh journey of insight and discovery into the amazing personal relationship with the Holy Spirit that is available to us.

1 Corinthians 2:9-10 says: *"But as it is written: 'Eye has not seen, nor ear heard, nor have entered into the heart of man the things which God has prepared for those who love Him.' But God has revealed them to us through His Spirit. For the Spirit searches all things, yes, the deep things of God."* What a powerful passage of Scripture this is. The things God has prepared for us He reveals to us by His Spirit! Since that is true, it is imperative you and I purpose to develop an intimate, personal relationship with the Holy Spirit. That is what this book will assist you to do.

When you spend time with the Holy Spirit, His voice and leading will become just as clear and distinct to you as the voice of one of your close family members. The truth is, Jesus is present with us in the person of the Holy Spirit 24/7. We need the Holy Spirit to teach us and lead us in God's plan for our lives. Jesus was filled with the Spirit, led by the Spirit, and followed the Holy Spirit throughout His life and ministry. If He needed the Holy Spirit, then how much more, do we?

We know that this book will be a great blessing and encouragement to you, as it has been to us. Thank you, Apostle Jacqueline, for being such a Gift to the Body of Christ, and for another wonderful book.

Dr Brad and Rev Wyona Norman
Apostolic Leaders & Founders
Salvation For The Nations International Churches

I have known Jacqui and family for many years now, and one thing about her has never changed: her desire to help people really encounter God. This latest book continues her aspiration. I have never heard anybody refer to the Holy Spirit as Heaven's Sherpa, but I have ministered in Nepal and heard incredible stories of the skill, courage and resilience found in Sherpa history. For the elevated, and sometimes dangerous terrain of Christian discipleship in our day, we need this Sherpa's help more than ever.

Read this book, not to duplicate the author's experience, but to discover your own! Believe on the Lord Jesus Christ, find deliverance and liberty in water baptism, and then receive the empowering baptism of the Holy Spirit. There is biblical evidence for you to know – beyond any doubt – that you have received Him. Next, follow Him closely through the directives of Scripture, and the gentle promptings He places in a prayerful heart. You will then find that Jacqui's testimony resonates in your soul, like an earthquake! May the power and presence of the Holy Spirit be a daily reality in your own walk with God, as you learn to know and trust Heaven's Sherpa.

Reverend Douglas C. Williams
Emmanuel Community Church International

I have known Jacqueline Peart for over 20 years, as a colleague, a pastor, and a cheerleader. In our early days, we worked together in discipleship and spiritual formation, learning to blend biblical theology on leadership with modern management mantras – an amazing journey that stretched us both. I have been privileged to proofread and reread her books. In all of them, there is the unmistakable "Jacqui brand" of "keeping it real"!

Jacqui has an almost effortless ability to bring life application to the text, and whilst this is not classical pneumatology (the theology of the Holy Spirit), this book is word-rich, and life-rich, with most theological principles lived out and simply exemplified in Jacqui's own life and ministry. You will be helped in understanding the text and seeing it modelled – a great methodology for effective mentoring. She tells, she shows, now you do...

You will read a plethora of textbooks on the Holy Spirit, but not many that you can live while learning (not all of us live and learn – some just live, some just learn). This book will inspire you to live and learn.

The concept of Heaven's Sherpa piqued my curiosity, and rewarded it well. It fits; it works. It will not replace biblical motifs such as fire, water and dove but it does exemplify and magnify these themes. Like all of Jacqui's books, it takes off and lands safely, but excitedly – and the mid-flight meal is substantial. I thoroughly enjoyed reading it, and found myself massively informed, and meaningfully challenged.

The section on pneumatology makes hard-core theology easier to swallow. Some people choke on the meat of truth, but Jacqui cuts our steak into bite-size truths, and by the time we are finished, we have a comprehensive grasp on the person, purpose, and work of the Holy Spirit. So, this book is a good access tool for understanding pneumatology.

I have worshipped and witnessed alongside Jacqui – she is for real and is well qualified to speak authoritatively on Heaven's Sherpa. I have seen her live these truths out through laughter and tears.

Well done Jacqui – I eagerly await the next 'theology for amateur mountaineers'.

Your brother from another mother, and fellow climber,

Pastor Anthony Hodgkinson (Pastor Antz)

It's an honour to be asked by Reverend Jacqueline Peart to recommend this book. I've known Jaqueline for over 20 years. As one of her first pastors, I can say that she is a genuine, lovable person and a woman of integrity that you can rely on. I love her teachable spirit; even when she knows more than you, she will listen.

Jacqueline came to our fellowship as a new believer with a willingness to learn and was diligent in completing any task that was given to her. Over the years, we prayed together, ate together, went walking together, and she instructed the leadership of the fellowship in team building and management. We were able to build a relationship that remained intact even after Jacqueline left our ministry, to the extent that when she was getting ordained, she insisted that I participate in the service.

Those who know Jacqueline are all supportive of her endeavours to accomplish the vision God has laid on her heart. "Heaven's Sherpa", what an analogy of the Holy Spirit! He is indeed our guide throughout our earthly journey. When we begin our walk with God, we are unaware of the difficulty of the road ahead or the dangers that we might encounter along the way. *The Holy Spirit…Heaven's Sherpa* has been given to us by the Father to assist us in every way, on our journey.

When I read what Jacqueline had to say about the Holy Spirit, my heart was moved. It stirred my spirit back to the time when God baptised me with the Holy Spirit and those earlier years of knowing and building a relationship with God the Father, the Son and the Holy Spirit.

It is necessary for young converts to understand that the most important thing in their walk is knowing whom they're walking with, and knowing who they are being led by.

This book not only has a good starting point for building a relationship with the Holy Spirit, but it also has great depth for growing and developing, creating lasting roots that will anchor, nourish, and support you throughout your walk with God.

For this reason, I can recommend this book even for those who have been on their journey for many years, especially since sometimes we find ourselves moving away from His direction and directives. It has happened to me: at times I have found that I am not walking in tandem with the leading of the Holy Spirit. We don't realise at times how far we have moved from

God until we read something like this book that reignites the fire that once burned within, the zeal that once made us want to convert the whole world to God!

It's never too late. God is waiting for us to get to know and follow the leading of the Holy Spirit, the One who has the knowledge, the direction and the power to accomplish any task and finish the journey. This book will give you insight into knowing and understanding the person of the Holy Spirit, our Guide and Companion for this journey.

Let's get started; He is waiting for us.

Pastor Veronica Joseph-Abrigo
Agape Tabernacle Ministries

Introduction

Why I wrote this book

I wrote this book because I sensed an urgent mandate from God to do so. As the end time stage is being set, I believe we need God's leadership and direction today and for the coming days more than ever before. The Holy Spirit is the Comforter and Help God has sent to equip and show us the way to go—and He is ready and willing to help. Given this significance, I seek to offer a practical guide, using the analogy of a Sherpa alongside biblical and modern-day examples of how we can truly be led by the Spirit. As Romans 8:14 states, *"For those who are led by the Spirit of God are the children of God."*

The Holy Spirit…Heaven's Sherpa has been written with two kinds of readers in mind. It is for those whose spiritual walk may have grown so mundane and powerless that they hunger to be stirred to delve deeper into their faith. These are believers who began running well but have stumbled into discouragement, distraction, or even derailment along the way. You can reignite and refresh your relationship with the Holy Spirit. You can restore that sense of excitement again—in fact, He is waiting for you to do that.

The second category of readers for whom this book is written are those who are yet to *fully* recognise the access they have to the Holy Spirit as born-again believers. They may not have appreciated just how loaded they are with His benefits and power. In fact, the Bible attests that the same Spirit that raised Jesus from the dead lives within us (Romans 8:11). There is no reason for believers to be living weak and powerless lives and yet, if the truth be told, many live just like that, day to day. Fear eclipses faith, doubt overshadows hope, control supersedes confidence, uncertainty displaces trust, and we live in a world that is doing its best to erase Jesus from the picture.

Well, I've got news for you—it's time for the true sons and daughters of God to arise. It's time to do the greater works spoken of by Jesus in John 14:12: *"Very truly I tell you, whoever believes in me will do the works I have been doing, and they will do even greater things than these, because I am going to the Father."*

Can I keep it real? Of all the books I have written to date, this one had me the most tentative and, paradoxically, the most excited. I have been tentative because of the differing opinions and doctrines surrounding the role of the Holy Spirit. Undoubtedly, there will be some who flat out disagree with my stance and even question the authenticity of my experiences with the Holy Spirit. If the truth be told, sometimes even I have questioned my experiences as I am left asking Heaven's Sherpa, "Did that really just happen?", when I know full well that it did. At the same time, I am also always excited because I know that encountering the Holy Spirit brings transformation, not just for us but also within our circle of influence and for those we are called to serve.

My desire in writing this book is to speak to those who yearn for a deeper, authentic and meaningful relationship with God, the Holy Spirit. Throughout the book, I will be sharing experiences of my walk with Him and retelling them as accurately as I can recall. In so doing, I pray that the Scriptures and accounts I share will resonate with your own experiences, validating that it was neither your imagination nor happenstance, but the work of the precious Holy Spirit.

On too many occasions, the glory for events orchestrated by the Holy Spirit has been given to luck, coincidence and happenstance. While I do not want us to get *"kooky"*, attributing everything that happens with some deep spiritual meaning, I do believe that God wants us to be open to cooperating with Him on a more consistent and intimate level.

When we shut ourselves off from being led by the Holy Spirit, we miss out on the fullness of who God is and the power available to us. I believe ailing to acknowledge, cooperate and partner with Him results in an incomplete experience of our faith.

Reflecting on the year 1995, when I first said "yes" to Jesus and committed to following Him, there was a lot of teaching about the Holy Spirit. Eager to learn more, I bought Benny Hinn's popular book, *Good Morning, Holy Spirit*. It was like a guiding light for people to begin to understand the person of the Holy Spirit. Back then, I believe people were open and hungry to hear about Him—they possessed an awareness of the Holy Spirit and keenness to fellowship with and know Him more deeply. However, over time, different waves have swept through the Church—some great, others unbalanced, a few even questionable—leaving behind not complete oblivion, but something akin to a shift in our longing, discernment and reliance upon Him. Some of these waves have been fleeting, but it is my firm belief that any movement genuinely orchestrated by God will remain.

The words of Gamaliel, an honoured Pharisee and teacher of the Law mentioned in the Bible, come to mind as they resonate with this notion. I love how he responded when Peter and the other Apostles refused to stop preaching in Jesus' name:

"Then he addressed the Sanhedrin: 'Men of Israel, consider carefully what you intend to do to these men. Some time ago Theudas appeared, claiming to be somebody, and about four hundred men rallied to him. He was killed, all his followers were dispersed, and it all came to nothing. After him, Judas the Galilean appeared in the days of the census and led a band of people in revolt. He too was killed, and all his followers were scattered. Therefore, in the present case I advise you: Leave these men alone! Let them go! For if their purpose or activity is of human origin, it will fail. But if it is from God, you will not be able to stop these men; you will only find yourselves fighting against God.'" Acts 5:35-39

Simply put, what is of God remains. His work cannot be halted, so let us not find ourselves on the wrong side fighting against Him.

With the unrelenting signs in this broken world, it is evident that we are living in end times and that our Lord and Saviour isn't far off in His second coming. If we are to see the prophesied harvest of souls that so many are believing for, then **WE NEED THE HOLY SPIRIT** to do the works that He has set for us to accomplish in Jesus' name. Through my careful study of the Scriptures and first-hand relationship with the Holy Spirit, it is my conviction that we need His power and guidance if we are going to make an impact on Earth.

I said earlier that I will be sharing experiences from my life and the lives of others so that you will know the Holy Spirit as a divine

Person, the third Person of the Trinity, and not as an impersonal force. I am sharing this so that you, too, can experience the counsel, the love, the guidance and the power of the Holy Spirit for yourself.

The journey to completion

As I was preparing this book for publication, I shared its structure with Rev. Denise Roberts, a respected colleague who I have worked and served with for over twenty years. She suggested that it would be beneficial to delve into greater detail about certain aspects of my journey mentioned in the introduction. I believe it was a nudge from the Holy Spirit as it resonated within my spirit to do so.

So here goes…

This is my eleventh book, or twelfth if we count a free 10-day devotional titled *10 Days of Inspiration*, available when you sign up to our mailing list. So, I have some experience of the various ways in which I will approach the writing process— from completing a project I had been working on for nearly ten years in four days after locking myself away in a hotel room, to emerging from one of my personal retreats with most of the content of another book that I didn't plan to write.

The Holy Spirit… Heaven's Sherpa began as a message I preached back in 2018. From that moment I have known that it needed to be turned into a book, but life and all its various priorities kept me from committing to the time to write it.

My sister, Rev. Yvonne Atkinson, or Coach V as she became affectionately known during the writing process (due to her calls and check-ins to see how I was proceeding), kept saying,

"We need the *Holy Spirit, Heaven's Sherpa*." Little did I know, two weeks before I started writing this book, that the Holy Spirit had a date in mind, because He had an assignment for it now.

On July 15, 2023, I was in a meeting to plan for a Masterclass I was going to be doing in New York on November 11, 2023. Part of the plan was to do a pre-event on the Friday evening before the Masterclass. As the planning committee went back and forth about how it could work, I began to feel unsure that it would be possible to do what I had hoped. Nevertheless, we agreed on a plan and the meeting concluded with a closing prayer. Then something unexpected happened. As the prayer was going forth, I heard that familiar unction of Heaven's Sherpa—"What about a book launch for the Friday evening?" I thought, "Erm… but I don't have a book to launch yet." As this internal conversation was going on, and before I could process what I was about to say, out of my mouth came, "How about a book launch?" I was surprised by my own words. However, everyone in the meeting was in favour and asked if I had a new book, to which I replied: "No, but I will."

I knew immediately that this was the Holy Spirit prompting me. I also knew the book you are now holding in your hands was the book waiting to be birthed. Despite what I had said, I was overcome with nerves and anticipation of how it would work and began wishing I hadn't committed myself to such a task.

Yet, if it's one thing I have learned about this walk with Heaven's Sherpa, He knows what we carry, He knows what He has put in us, and so He also knows what He can pull out of us for the glory of God. He knows, even when we do not.

The first thing I did was to clear my diary so I could focus solely on writing. Over the next two weeks, I sat at home in the quiet of our living room, day after day, morning to evening, the Holy Spirit leading, nudging and speaking to me as I wrote. Throughout this period, I recalled encounters from my life before I became a Christian to the moment I said yes. I pored over Scripture after Scripture to make sure I presented the Holy Spirit biblically and with integrity. I paused to recognise some of the leaders who have been role models in my life, walking in step and being guided by the Holy Spirit, Heaven's Sherpa. The process of writing this book has been one that has inspired, encouraged, and challenged me all over again to follow where the Holy Spirit leads.

I have not been the only witness to the guidance of the Holy Spirit during the time of writing. My mum and sister Marcia can also testify how things just kept falling into place— even during times of frustration, there was victory or lessons to be learned. Many times, we stopped and praised God in the small and large events, and it has been refreshing.

The process took on a beautiful flow as I wrote—do not get me wrong, there were challenges along the way, but nothing that could stop me from writing or hinder my peace or joy for too long.

After I completed the book, I revisited the introduction because I had bookmarked a section with the initials "HS" to remind me to include something additional about the Holy Spirit. Right then, I realised Heaven's Sherpa and the Holy Spirit share the same initials. I am not sure if that is relevant or not, what I do know is that this beautiful synchronicity made me smile.

What I hadn't reckoned on—even though I had prayed for a fresh encounter—was a renewed sense of closeness to God through the Holy Spirit while writing. I felt His presence and unction in such a fresh, tangible way that uplifted my heart. The only way I can describe it is like cleaning your dusty or smeared glasses and being surprised at how much sharper your vision is. I am seeing Him clearer, leaning on Him more closely and hearing Him more sharply. I have been reminded of how obedience in the smallest matters reaps great rewards.

Let me give you an example. One night, as I lay in bed, I sensed the Holy Spirit bidding me to check in on my mum. I looked at the time and it was 11.40 pm, so I said, "She'll be sleeping," and turned over to go to sleep. Immediately, I felt convicted, so I said, "Sorry, Holy Spirit, I'll go." To my surprise, there she was in the dark on her phone, shopping online with her headphones on. I said, "What are you doing up this late?" Mum giggled and so did I, then she asked, "How did you know I was up?" I said the Holy Spirit told me. Oh, how it made us both laugh. This may not be a big thing to someone else but for me, it meant several things: firstly, it was another opportunity to enjoy my mum and, secondly, it was a moment to repent and say, "Holy Spirit, You know everything, so even in the smallest things, I will follow." That night, I went to bed laughing my way to sleep.

Amidst the stories and teachings shared within these pages, I believe the anecdote I just recounted serves as a vivid reminder of the Holy Spirit's intimate involvement in even the seemingly mundane moments of our lives.

As you journey through this book, my prayer is that you sense the powerful and intense presence of the Holy Spirit in moments just like this and more. I pray He encounters you right where you are—whether on the train, in your living room or bedroom, on your job or on holiday. I pray this book lights a fire and desire within you that says, "I NEED YOU, HOLY SPIRIT—I'M READY

TO COOPERATE WITH YOU AND BE LED BY YOU LIKE NEVER BEFORE!"

I pray you experience the supernatural power, love and presence of a God who is alive and desires a relationship with you!

I pray your heart and your ears are open to hear what the Spirit of the Lord will say to you. I pray that as you encounter Him afresh, your life will be undeniably marked and transformed!

Are you ready?

Then let us begin a fresh journey within the School of the Holy Spirit.

Oh, just before we do, I want to ask you to do one thing for me. As you encounter the Holy Spirit, please drop me an email or reach out to me via social media. I want to marvel at His goodness with you. My contact details are at the back of the book.

Now, Holy Spirit, our guide, Heaven's Sherpa here on Earth, lead us into all truth. In Jesus' name. Amen.

SECTION ONE
My Early Encounters with the Holy Spirit

1

Meeting the Holy Spirit

Jesus says in John 6:44,
"No one can come to me, unless the
Father who sent me, draws them, and
I will raise them at the last day."

My first encounters with the Holy Spirit began before I realised it. He had been drawing me for many years unknown to my conscious self.

The Greek word for "draw" in John 6:44 is "*helko*" and means to drag or draw with an emphasis on being led by the One who is doing the dragging. According to *Strong's*, the word "*helko*" is used eight times in the New Testament and also refers to the dragging or drawing of a sword (John 18:10); and the dragging or drawing of a catch of fish (John 21:6,11).

This demonstrates that it is God who does the drawing. It means that during all the times before I finally said "yes" to the Lord, the Holy Spirit was drawing and dragging me. As I began to research why we have to be drawn or dragged into the Kingdom, I consulted Got Questions Ministries, which gave me the following response to the question, "Why does God need to draw us to Salvation?"

"Simply put, if He didn't, we would never come. Jesus explains that no man can come unless He draws him (John 6:65). The natural man has no ability to come to God, nor does he even have the desire to come. Because his heart is hard and his mind is darkened, the unregenerate person doesn't desire God and is actually an enemy of God (Romans 5:10)."

I concur with that; the world and all its trappings seem so appealing. The strategy of hell is to keep us looking at what we can physically see instead of what is unseen and in the realm of the spirit, which keeps many away from experiencing an abundant life in Christ.

As a child, my parents ensured we went to Sunday School, so I knew about Jesus, but I didn't have a relationship with Him yet. In fact, as soon as I was old enough to choose, I stopped going to Sunday School. I was drawn to the world and what it seemed to offer, and that included going to nightclubs and all that entailed.

Proverbs 22:6 says, *"Train up a child in the way he should go; when he is old he will not depart from it"* (NKJV). True to the word, no matter how much I attempted to fit into the world's model, there was always something holding me back from going too far. I believe it's because I had been trained in the way of the Lord as a child, and so even when I got into sticky situations, I knew to pray, even if they were selfish prayers. I would pray something like, "God, please get me out of this" or "Help me get home" or "Help me to get that job." In hindsight, all of this was God's drawing me to Himself, teaching me to trust Him even when I didn't fully understand what it meant to have a relationship with Him.

Between 1993 and 1994, a dear friend of mine, who I had met while working for Wandsworth Council, began inviting me to church events and talking to me about Jesus. Her name was Magdalene, and the things she spoke about weren't unusual to me because of the days I had spent in Sunday School. Magdalene continually drip-fed invitations and insights about the Lord but I wasn't ready to hear it at all because I was still in the world. At the time, I was dating someone who had long-term potential, so the idea of changing my lifestyle wasn't on my agenda.

There were several of us in the council office who got on well and encouraged each other. We would go to lunch and spend time together outside the workplace. On one occasion, there was a deejay and sound system coming to a pub near where we worked. A couple of us joked about inviting Magdalene, knowing that she wouldn't come because she was a Christian. Well, we invited her and to our surprise, she agreed to come. This baffled me and I was thinking, "She talks so much about Jesus and she's coming to the pub for the Sound Clash (two sound systems competing with each other)?"

When we got to the pub, I ordered a Vodka and Coke, and my friend ordered her drink. I do not remember what Magdalene drank, but it was something non-alcoholic. I can still remember how uncomfortable Magdalene looked while myself and the others danced away to the music. I had no intention of sharing this but as I began musing about my first encounter, I was reminded of this moment. It sowed a seed in my life because I knew that Magdalene had stepped out of her comfort zone to be a witness.

I am not sharing this to justify going into nightclubs and pubs under the guise of witnessing to a friend. I believe this woman of God was on an assignment from God. If you believe God has given you a similar assignment to go to the clubs and pubs, God bless you—go with His covering and the blessing of your leadership. If it just sounds like a *good* idea, then I would strongly suggest you pause until you know it is a *GOD* idea.

Soon after this nightclub event, I got another job at another local authority, but I stayed in contact with Magdalene as we had become good friends. In my next job, there were several other Christians who also presented themselves with invitations, insights, and encouragement. Although I tried to resist, the dragging of the Spirit continued, drawing me closer and closer.

Being drawn by the Holy Spirit through a house purchase

I had been house hunting on and off for several years without success and so I began to squander my deposit on things that do not last, like socialising. Then, out of the blue, a house came up that looked like what I had been searching for. While it wasn't quite the area I had been looking for, when I went to look at it, the location seemed like a good one.

When I checked my bank account to see where I was with my savings, I realised how little was left. I was sharing this with Magdalene one day when she asked, "Have you prayed about it?" I was thinking, "*Pray about it?* I need hard cash, not prayers!" Seeing my frustration, she encouraged me and said that if I believed, God could make a way, so I should pray.

If I'm honest, I was irritated because it wasn't what I wanted to hear, yet somehow something about it struck a chord within me. Even so, I decided to make it happen another way. I went to the Bank of Mum and Dad and asked to borrow some money. Wrong move. Mum wasn't too pleased to hear that I didn't have enough in my savings to pay the deposit. I later found out that she wanted to buy me something for the house, not contribute to the deposit. I was running out of options and the estate agent was pressing for an answer as to whether this was the house for me or not.

At the time, I was doing some freelance work so I started to put the feelers out to see if I could get any additional contracts to raise the funds I needed, but nothing seemed to work.

Out of my usual options, I returned home from work one day, went up to my room, shut the door and I got on my knees. I began to pray. Initially, I started to pray about the house and then something changed. I found myself saying, "Lord, if you're real, if you're really real, I want to know You." It wasn't a fancy, three or two-steps to Salvation prayer, but it was all that I had. As I began to weep, I sensed what felt like a refreshing or cleansing. Something was happening in my room though I didn't know how to articulate it at the time. I just knew I was sorry, and I needed Him.

A prayer for a physical house made of bricks and mortar led to a prayer about a human temple made of flesh (1 Corinthians 6:19). It was time to surrender to God.

This encounter, and Magdalene's words that "if I believed, God would make a way", were enough for me to tell the estate agent that I wanted to go ahead with the purchase of the house—a move that was alien to me because I like to know how things are going to happen and what is needed. However, when I arose to my feet, I felt peace, so I engaged a solicitor, put in an offer, which was accepted, and prepared myself as the time of completion drew near. I do not know how I had so much peace, but I do know it could only have been God.

A few days before I had to pay my deposit and fees, I returned home from work and there were several letters in the post for me. I opened the first one and it was payment for some freelance work I had facilitated. I opened the next envelope, and there was a cheque for £300 from my aunt. She had heard I was buying a house and wanted to bless me. I rushed up the stairs to tell my mum, because I was excited by the way it was all coming together, but before I could say a word, she handed me a cheque that was enough to pay the deposit.

Recalling this time makes me feel overwhelmed all over again. I didn't know I was being dragged and drawn by the Holy Spirit to the Father but I was starting to realise that something was happening because, without a shadow of a doubt, I knew it could not have been anyone else. Had the money come in dribs and drabs, I would have been guilty of praising luck and coincidence, but the way everything lined up with precision and timing, I knew it was God.

Meanwhile, I was still friends with Magdalene. She invited me to her church again and this time, I accepted the invitation. When I went, I was blown away by the worship. I began to cry as a couple sang. I formally accepted Jesus as my Lord and Saviour at that service. I say "formally", because I believe that the night I prayed in my room, I had answered the purest "yes" to following Jesus I could give.

The drawing of the Holy Spirit was bearing fruit and I was on my way to being sold out for Jesus.

If the truth be known, I accepted Jesus as my Lord and Saviour many times after that. Each time I went to a service from that moment on and heard an altar call, I would say "yes"—I just wanted to make sure I was saved!

This experience was the first time I was conscious of an encounter with the Holy Spirit. Shortly after this, I purchased the house and the whole adventure was undoubtedly a God intervention. You might think that would be all I needed to fully follow Jesus, but, as I mentioned before, I was in a relationship, and I wasn't ready to let that go. What I didn't realise at the time was that the persistent Holy Spirit wasn't ready to let go of me either. I decided to seek God over the relationship. I asked God to clearly show me if this was the man for me. I said that whatever the outcome I would serve Him. Well, through a simple misdirection of priorities on my boyfriend's part, it became evident that he wasn't the one God had for me, so I ended the relationship, honoured my word, and began to serve Jesus once and for all.

That was January 1995, and I have not looked back. I have not stopped or quit the race, even though there have been many times when the pressures and battles have had me near to the brink of saying enough is enough.

A dove in my room

Months after moving into my new house, while I was in my bedroom getting ready for bed, I heard a sound like huge wings flapping. I was immediately scared but then it stopped, so I put it down to "new-house" sounds and settled into bed.

In the early hours of the morning, as the daylight filtered into the room, I was in between sleeping and waking when I heard the sound again. This time, I saw what appeared to be a dove fly into my room. It was translucent, and when I looked again it was gone. The most significant memory from this experience was the sound of those wings; they were deep and echoey, like nothing of this world. My first thought was, "What was that!" For a split second I felt afraid but then this sense of peace came over me and I drifted back asleep. As a new believer, I had no idea of the significance of the dove. Later, I shared it with Magdalene and she asked me if I had received the baptism of the Holy Spirit. "No," I said, "what's that?" There and then in her living room she laid hands on me and began to pray that I would receive the baptism of the Holy Spirit. As she prayed, I began to stutter some new words that made no sense, yet as I continued to stutter and eventually speak with 'new tongues', a deep joy came over me. That evening, I drove from Magdalene's home in Hounslow to my home in East London laughing, crying and stammering in awe of the words coming out of my mouth.

Over the years, I have had many more encounters with the Holy Spirit—how about you? It would be wonderful if you paused for a moment to acknowledge the Holy Spirit who has drawn you to Christ. This would be a perfect opportunity to give thanks for His leading, His guiding and, most of all, His drawing and dragging.

For those who are reading this today who have not yet encountered the Holy Spirit and have not accepted Jesus Christ as your Lord and Saviour, there is no time like the present.

Turn to the back of this book and pray the prayer of salvation, inviting Jesus into your heart. I believe reading this book is the Holy Spirit's way of drawing you to Christ. Find a quiet space and with your whole heart pray the prayer on the page, knowing that God has been wooing you to Himself. Today is your day!

An act of obedience – baptism

After committing my life to the Lord, I sought a home church where I could grow and learn more about this God who loved the world so much that He sent His only begotten Son to die for our sins (John 3:16). I had been travelling from East London to South Kensington and the journey after a couple of months was becoming arduous, preventing me from making the midweek meetings because of the distance. Magdalene suggested I pray about finding a church that would be right for me in my local area. So, I did.

I had worked in a restaurant at a nightclub for about a year and got to know the deejays, the bouncers and some of the regulars. One of the deejays called, inviting me to a party and offering to leave my name on the guest list if I wanted to come. It was the first time I had heard from him since I had become a Christian. I remember feeling nervous, knowing I had to tell him I had given my life to Jesus Christ and would no longer be raving. When I told him that my life had changed, he was more understanding than I had expected. I mentioned that I needed to find a church near to me and he told me about a friend of his called Samantha who was attending one not far from where I lived. He said he would give her my details. A couple of weeks later, Samantha called and invited me to her church, which was less than two miles from where I was living. God had answered my prayer.

The first time I walked into the service, I felt such an amazing sense of love, peace and joy as the praise and worship team sang. I immediately knew this was home. I attended regularly and signed up for baptism classes, sensing that would be the next step in my faith journey. I like to understand the reasons behind what I'm doing, rather than doing it because someone says I should do this or do that. So, although I knew baptism was what Christians do, I questioned why I needed to get baptised. When I learned that it was a public demonstration of my faith, I was like, "Well everyone who knows me, knows without a shadow of a doubt I am fully sold out to the Lord, so why do I need to go under the water?"

During our pre-baptism classes, I continued to ask questions, not to be awkward, but because I genuinely wanted to understand. "Why do I need to get baptised, if I've already made a public declaration?" One evening, I left the class frustrated because I just didn't understand. I was shown it was in the Bible (Matthew 28:19; Mark 16:16; Acts 2:38), and that even Jesus Himself was baptised (Matthew 3:16), yet something wasn't sitting right. I was still pondering this while going ahead with my preparations to be baptised when I heard a soft voice within say, "It's out of obedience." Immediately, the peace I had become acquainted with returned and I knew it was the Holy Spirit answering my question.

After this encounter, everything started to fall into place. I was dying to self and being raised with Christ. I was ready.

Can I just say, one word from the Lord changes everything. If I hadn't received that revelation about obedience, I would still have been baptised—ironically, out of obedience—however, that nagging question would have remained. God knew this, and this experience became one of my earliest recollections of the Holy Spirit nudging me towards clarity and teaching me what Jesus had said in Scripture.

"But the Advocate, the Holy Spirit, whom the Father will send in my name, will teach you all things and will remind you of everything I have said to you." (John 14:26)

Learning to Walk with the Holy Spirit

The more I followed the promptings in my heart, backed up by the Scriptures, the more I was learning to recognise the voice of the Holy Spirit. I was growing in confidence that He was leading me. As you can imagine, this was an extremely exciting as well as new experience for me. It was like transitioning from groping around in the dark to find my way forward in life to suddenly having a consistently reliable source of light to guide my path. That didn't mean I didn't make mistakes or, at times, question whether what I was hearing was coming from self or Spirit. But I was learning to walk with the Holy Spirit and to see that those moments of questioning and uncertainty were part of the process of growing to trust Heaven's Sherpa.

Was she an angel?

The day of my baptism finally arrived in August 1995, and I was nervous yet ready. I had invited over a hundred friends, family and colleagues in the hope that some of them would come and hear the gospel. I was on a mission to see all the people I knew come to know Jesus as their Lord and Saviour.

There was a full house of guests who had come to support the baptismal candidates. When my turn came, I emerged from the water with a mighty shout of 'hallelujah'. It was a glorious time, yet I felt a little disappointed. I had heard stories of how people experienced something supernatural, like seeing visions or prophesying, when they were baptised. I wanted that too and had prayed asking the Lord to do something supernatural for me. Do not get me wrong, I was full and revived as I was baptised, but I just longed for something more.

One of the other people being baptised was my friend Anthony. He owned a pub and club at the time, so we agreed to invite both of our groups of guests to the hall at his venue to celebrate our decision. Looking back at this makes me smile—the place we had both come out of (clubs and pubs) was the place we chose to celebrate our change of life. We had become new creations (2 Corinthians 5:17).

The refreshments we served included some non-alcoholic wine. I was being hostess and pouring the wine into glasses for our guests. While I was filling one glass, the person jolted her hand and the wine started to spill. I looked up and saw a mature woman, short in stature with her hair in a bun, wearing a sparkly sequin top. I can still remember her and some of her features. I gestured to her to be careful, and she smiled with what seemed like a twinkle in her eye. Later that evening, I saw her sitting next to a couple of my friends, but I didn't think any more of it. We had a beautiful celebration and then we all left for our respective homes.

That night, lying in bed, I began to muse with the Lord on the day. Whispering, I told the Lord that I had hoped for a supernatural experience during my baptism like I had heard others had. Once again, I heard a soft voice within me saying, "Who said I didn't?"

I was puzzled because I thought I knew exactly what happened during my baptism and didn't see any signs of anything supernatural—you know, like blind eyes opening or the deaf hearing. Immediately, the lady whose glass I filled and her smile came to mind. I began to question who she was. The next day, I called the two people she was sitting next to, and they said they hadn't noticed her. I called family members and my friend whose venue we were at, and no one could recall this woman. I began to think, "Was she an angel?"

When I studied angelology (doctrine of angels), I realised that God does not just send angels on non-essential missions. To this day, I believe He did send an angel. It opened my heart to more of Him and what He would do. It boosted my faith, which, to be honest, wasn't difficult because I was in a place of simply wanting to be all God had called me to be. Our God is amazing!

Praying Holy Spirit-led prayers

That first house I bought taught me so much about walking with the Lord. Those early years of my faith were littered with encounters that have grounded me, kept me and led me right up to this day.

The Bible tells us that *"the Spirit helps us in our weakness. We do not know what we ought to pray for, but the Spirit himself intercedes for us through wordless groans"* (Romans 8:26). There have been multiple times when I have said prayers I had no idea that I was going to pray, and many times I have prayed without realising how impactful it would be afterwards. For example, I recall being at home in my bedroom praying. As I prayed, I began to cry out to the Lord because I knew that there was more to be experienced. Can I keep it real? I was starting to question how it was that we serve such an omnipotent, all-powerful, faithful, loving God, yet it seemed like many Christians lacked the joy of the Lord. There was conflict, gossip, cliques and more, and I just wanted Jesus in a deeper way. As I prayed, I began to move from what I was seeing to who and where I was. I began to ask God to "make me whole, make me who You created me to be". This was in 1997.

I had no idea where that prayer came from and I didn't fully understand what "make me whole" meant. It just seemed to flow out of me as I prayed earnestly. Fast forward more than 25 years later and my heart continues to burn for people to become whole. I long for the body of Christ to find its security in God alone; find identity in Jesus our Lord and Saviour; and have an intimate relationship with God the Father, through Jesus Christ. When we do, we find ourselves walking in our God-ordained purpose and calling.

What a transformed world this would be if we allowed the Holy Spirit to lead and guide us consistently. Not stopping and starting, not when it's convenient for us, not when it makes sense to us, but day by day, moment by moment, humbling ourselves and allowing His Spirit to lead. This world would become a place where brokenness is healed by the love of God as each person surrenders. A world where denominations and Christian organisations preach and teach Jesus at every opportunity they get. A world where the fruit, gifts and ministries of the Holy Spirit are not debated but welcomed, and the body of Christ boldly marches forward as children of God.

The Holy Spirit helps me to pray and He helps you to pray, when we let Him. Even when it makes no sense to us, He knows what He is doing. I have learned over the years, and I am still learning, that God sees around corners, and we do not. He sees across nations simultaneously, and we cannot. So, when we are led to pray prayers that we hadn't intended to, we may never know the impact they are having somewhere else.

I remember hearing a story about a man who, while camping on a mission trip to a country unfamiliar to him, was surrounded by natives of the country, who were planning to attack him and his small team. At the same time, a small village church back in the UK was holding a prayer meeting. As they prayed, one of the intercessors felt a strong urgency to pray for someone on mission in the same country as that missionary. Just as his attackers were about to strike, they began to disperse one by one. One of the attackers, who later gave his life to the Lord, told the missionary of the plot to attack him that day. When the missionary asked why they hadn't attacked, the would-be attacker said, "Just as we were about to, we saw you surrounded by men with flames and swords around the camp. We quickly retreated shocked because we had heard there were just a few of you."

I do not know how the intercessors and missionary came to meet and exchange stories, but they did. When they began to exchange accounts of the evening and put the times together of when this had happened, they realised that the attack was thwarted at about the same time they had begun to pray. There were 12 people praying and it was said that there were 12 people that were trying to attack the missionary. Think about that, and what power your prayers have when they are led by the Holy Spirit. Think about the power we have within us that we so often override with common sense, logic and programmes based on what we have always done, or think should be done.

I want to pause here to encourage someone. I believe the Holy Spirit has been speaking to you and leading you to pray about matters that seem strange to you but are necessary to the plans of God. You have felt uncomfortable sharing this with others because the enemy has made you think that it is in your mind. You think you will be misunderstood or not taken seriously if you share it. I want to encourage you—if everything makes perfect sense, why do we need God? If we look at our Saviour's track record, He was frequently misunderstood and questioned about what He said and the claims He made. His Identity was challenged. Many people in Jesus' time, and to this day, misunderstand His true identity. Some thought He was merely a prophet or a great teacher, while others believed He might be John the Baptist or one of the prophets returned from the dead. It wasn't until later in Jesus' ministry that His disciples recognised Him as the long-awaited Messiah and the Son of God (Matthew 16:13-17).

So, what Jesus said and taught was at times misunderstood, not only by religious leaders who were often critical of Jesus' interpretations of the Law, purely because they saw it as a challenge to their authority, but also by His own disciples. At times, they failed to grasp the underlying messages Jesus taught through parables, which were meant to convey a deeper meaning (Mark 4:10-13).

When Jesus revealed His divine nature and His unity with the Father, stating that He and the Father are one, some of the religious leaders misunderstood what He meant and claimed He was blaspheming. They accused Him of claiming to be God, which led to conflicts and attempts to arrest Him (John 10:30-31).

There are many more examples of others who were misunderstood, like the Apostle Paul, Peter and even Stephen, the first Christian to be martyred by stoning. These individuals were led by the Holy Spirit to pray prayers that in our human minds, we wouldn't think about. Yet when we are filled and led by the Spirit, these prayers flow out of that relationship with God. How do I know this? Consider Stephen who, whilst being accused of blasphemy and about to be stoned, gave an accurate and clear history lesson of God's dealings with Abraham and his descendants, then rebuked those about to stone him, calling them "stiff-necked" for resisting the Holy Spirit, and then forgave his murderers in his final moments. Read his account in Acts 7. I believe Stephen was able to pray Holy Spirit-led prayers and make such an impact because He was "full of the Holy Spirit" (Acts 7:55).

How many times have we overridden the voice and the leading of the Holy Spirit, putting it down to our imagination, or eating too much cheese the night before? The Holy Spirit is real, and He wants to lead you. He wants to direct, counsel, comfort and infuse you with power. The Holy Spirit wants you to trust Him.

I pray you will continue to pray prayers that are led by the Holy Spirit. Even when you do not understand, He does. As long as your prayers align with Scripture, pray as you are led. If you have been a Christian for any length of time, you will know that misunderstandings and challenges to our faith and how we live it out, are part of the journey.

A poet and I didn't know it

In 1997, my family and I had the opportunity to go on holiday to the Algarve in Portugal. It was the first time in many years that we had all been together since my oldest sister had emigrated to the United States of America. We walked, we talked, we laughed, we ate and we went to the beach. It was a wonderful time. It blessed my heart so much that I whispered a prayer of "thank You" to the Holy Spirit. "Whatever You want me to do, I'm available," I prayed. A couple of days later, I had such a strong urge to find a pen and some paper. We were staying in a tourist area so these were not the easiest things to find—beach balls, flip flops, buckets and spades, yes, but a notebook, no.

I eventually found a shop that sold notepads. I found an A5 one with light blue and white stripes across the front and cardboard at the back. All the time I was looking for the notepad and pen, I had no idea why. However, I remembered the prayer I had prayed a few days earlier thanking God and saying that I would do whatever He wanted me to do. We arrived at the beach, and just as I was about to lie down to relax, words that sounded like poetry began coming to me. I quickly sat up and began writing the words I received. The first poem I wrote was called, "You Can!" and based on Philippians 4:13.

You Can!

©Taken from In Search of Wholeness and A S.A.F.E. Place Journal… For Women

What happens when you think you can't?

You can

What happens when you believe you can't?

You can

What happens when everyone else....................

You can

What happens when you....................................

You can

But what if you've................................

You can

What happens when I really just can't?

HE CAN!

God was just waiting for you to cast your can't onto Him so YOU CAN!

This simple poetic inspiration highlights the fact that no matter what is going on in your life, you can overcome it, you can do it. God is so often just waiting for you to cast your "can'ts" onto Him, so you can. I loved it and just kept writing as another came, then another. I shared the poems with my family, and they were just as surprised as I was. After writing like a ready writer led by the Holy Spirit, I left the beach with over a dozen poems.

That day, I realised that I was a poet, and I didn't know it. When I returned to the UK from holiday, I met up with a friend for a shopping trip in London's West End and told her about this experience of writing poetry. She wasn't a Christian but asked to hear one of my poems. I immediately obliged, took out my notepad and read her one that I refer to as my Testimony Poem, called "Looking for Me". As I read it, she became noticeably quiet, so I assumed she didn't think much of it. Then I realised why—she was crying. She said, "That sums up exactly where I am right now, how did you know?" I thought, wow—only God!

Looking for Me

©Taken from In Search of Wholeness and Inspirations for Women… A Journey to Wholeness

Has anyone found me?
I'm looking for me!

I'm a little girl masquerading as a woman.

I got lost along the way, wanting to be all for everyone, leaving none for me.

Anyone found me?
I'm looking for me!

I'm a mother, a lover, a sister, a friend, all my different roles I
play so very well,
An Oscar winner I could be.

But has anyone found me, the real me?
Because I'm looking for me!
I'm professional, I'm witty, some say charming as well.
But has anyone seen me?
I'm looking for me!

Like a pressure cooker, I'll explode if I don't find me soon.
Has anyone found me? I'm looking for me...

God speaks... Ssssssh my child,

Before you were born, I named you and ordained you.
Rest with Me a while, for My yoke is easy and My burden is light.

You are who I say you are.
When you search for me with your whole heart, you'll find the
Me you're looking for.
I found Me.

These words became a bridge to a friend who needed the touch of the Lord in her life. Shortly after this encounter, I met with her and her husband and he gave his life to the Lord while she took one more step towards truly knowing Him, not just knowing of Him. The gift of writing, unbeknownst to my flesh, had been lying dormant within me, awaiting my obedience to His leading to manifest. This may not seem like a big thing for some reading this, but for me it was. I had failed my English Literature exams in school, I wasn't a writer and, can I keep it real? I didn't like poetry--it seemed boring to me. Yet, here I was writing it. I eventually published the poetry I was writing in a series of seven books called, "Inspirations for..."

The gift of poetry opened doors for me across denominations, generations, cultures, counties and even nations. Doors in the media were opened to me on television and radio, locally and abroad. It was during a poetry reading at a church during a women's conference that I was connected with some amazing leaders. They played a pivotal role in the next part of my destiny, which included speaking, preaching and, ultimately, being ordained.

All of this flowed from being led to finding a pen and a notepad on holiday. Likewise, the Holy Spirit knows what is lying deep within you. He knows what gifts and talents are waiting to be birthed because He is the One that distributes them to whom He pleases for the glory of God, as described in 1 Corinthians 12:4-6.

Why have I included all these examples of times when I believe I was led by the Holy Spirit? Because I believe someone reading this right now has had experiences that they have questioned, thinking somehow that they do not make sense. As I write and recount these experiences from over twenty-five years ago, I marvel at how God the Holy Spirit has been leading me all this time. No doubt, some may find it difficult to comprehend; and if you do, this is the exact reason why you need the Holy Spirit— only He can lead you into all truth. Only He can light up the way of the Spirit. I believe the Holy Spirit is nudging, whispering, unctioning, leading, directing, alerting, and desiring that you know Him in both the small and large things.

God is God, and the more we try to fathom His mysteries, the more we become entangled in logic. I am good with letting

God be God. I am good with allowing Him to be bigger than my finite mind. I am good with letting Him lead. How about you?

Have a break

As part of my journey learning to walk with the Holy Spirit, hear His voice, and follow His leading, He was also teaching me to hear Him and His unctioning through other people. There were times I would sit in services and wonder how the speaker knew what I was thinking or what I had been going through. Only as the years went by, I began to understand that it was the Holy Spirit's enabling of each speaker to speak prophetically and profoundly into the hearts of the listeners.

I remember vividly going through an extremely busy season during those early days when one night I had a dream. In the dream, I was standing outside looking up towards the sky, and there was a tiny parachute winging its way to me with a famous brand of chocolate bar attached to it. The dream was so clear that I kept pondering what it meant. The Holy Spirit led me to a prophet in the church who was adept at interpreting dreams, so I shared the dream with him, and he began to laugh. I was puzzled, until he gave the interpretation. The chocolate bar has a slogan that includes the words "have a break". I remember being totally in awe of the fact that God cared about my well-being so much that He would send me such a dream. He also knew I would be inquisitive enough to want to know what the dream meant and then allowed this prophet to speak as the Holy Spirit gave Him utterance.

I do not know who this is for, but I am fully persuaded that the Holy Spirit wants to encourage someone to rest. How do I know that? Because this example wasn't included in the first draft of the finished manuscript but added after the book had been edited and reached the typesetting stage. Right then, I felt convinced that someone reading this in the future would need to hear this. You have been running on empty and God knows that, so the Holy Spirit intervened in the final moments of the book production process to let you know, "IT'S TIME TO TAKE A BREAK."

I love how the Holy Spirit moves; what seems like an interruption or late input to my printing timetable is His divine appointment for you. IT IS OKAY TO REST, IT IS OKAY TO PAUSE, IT IS OKAY! When the Holy Spirit is speaking to you through someone else, it will bear witness with your spirit, and it will NEVER contradict the Scriptures.

Selah… Pause and think on this as we continue to explore more encounters with the Holy Spirit in the next Section.

SECTION TWO
One Encounter with the Holy Spirit

3

One Encounter with the Holy Spirit Changes Things

I firmly believe and have witnessed how one touch, one word, one encounter with God has the power to change a person's life. There have been many occasions in my life when I have needed the Holy Spirit to help me make an important decision, and there have been other times when I've been unaware of my need to decide on a course of action until the Holy Spirit revealed it. That's the beautiful thing about Heaven's Sherpa— He is constantly watching out for us and causing us to "know the way we should go". I would like to share some of the key moments in my life when the Holy Spirit has done just that.

Preaching and teaching about the Holy Spirit

On August 5, 2018, I preached a message on the Holy Spirit to the launch team of the International Wholeness Centre (IWC), an Equipping Centre and church I planted in East London with the help of a leadership team. As I stood up to preach, something unexpected happened—I began to sing a new song. Although singing isn't my primary gift, there was such a sweet sound as

I sang. Within moments, an outpouring of praise and worship ignited in the house that awoke every sleepy and weary heart.

I began to preach about the Holy Spirit—who He is, His names, why He came, and His gifts and attributes. His presence was so tangible as I preached and taught that there were times I was simply overwhelmed. We continued the message during our Thursday night Bible study because there was still so much to learn. As I picked up on the teaching, the Holy Spirit showed up once again. There was a young man in the meeting, who we will call James, who had been a member of the Jehovah's Witness faith. James had committed his life to Jesus Christ and was renewing his mind to the things of God. I do not recall how it happened, but before we knew it, James began to speak in tongues. There was no travailing at the altar, just the natural spontaneous utterance of a new language for one of God's children. We were in awe of God witnessing this. I saw how things can change simply through teaching others about the Holy Spirit.

The following month, I had the honour of preaching at a worship retreat and as I was seeking the Lord about what to preach, He directed me to speak on the Holy Spirit. I'm always mindful of preaching and teaching doctrine in new places because I know that differing beliefs can be a divider. I waited and prayed but the Holy Spirit's prompting didn't change: "Teach and preach on the Holy Spirit… Heaven's Sherpa." Well, I did. I ministered as I was led and the Holy Spirit's presence felt tangible. I opened the altar for those who wanted to be filled by or draw closer to the Holy Spirit, and people began to move seamlessly in one accord towards the altar. Some wept, some fell to their knees and others cried out to God. It was a beautiful sight to witness.

Years later, I caught up with the event's host and as we reflected on how powerful that day was, he also shared that before the event, some people had been asking him who I was. They were used to having some of the most prominent pastors and preachers in the nation speak at their events so wanted to know where I was from. The host said after that event, no one questioned why I had been invited. The same Holy Spirit leading me had led him to invite me and God had spoken for Himself.

One encounter with the Lord changes everything.

Later during that same month of September 2018, Jacqueline Peart International Ministries (JPIM) hosted an annual retreat, a gathering we had been facilitating for over ten years. As always, I enquired of the Lord what to preach and once again, He said, "Teach on the Holy Spirit." Again, throughout and as the preaching concluded, the sense of His manifest presence was undeniable. People were healed (including physical healing), delivered and filled with the Spirit. One person, who was a pastor, asked for prayer as she wanted to receive the gift of speaking in tongues. After the team and I prayed for her and she was preparing to leave, she mentioned that she still hadn't received the gift of speaking in the spiritual language. Immediately, I sensed the Holy Spirit saying, "Reassure her that even if it is in bed at home, she will indeed speak in tongues." I shared this with her, and we all went our separate ways. Sure enough, a few days later I received a voice message from her, crying, praising and speaking in tongues...

Hallelujah!

One encounter with the Holy Spirit changes everything.

Why is my heart always breaking?

I was still relatively young in my faith, but the more I trusted and followed His voice, the more I learned how to recognise and walk in alignment with the Holy Spirit's continuous guidance. One afternoon, I was invited for a meal at the home of a family from church. A few of the other congregants and the assistant pastor were also present. I had been feeling discouraged about various events that had been taking place and, while we were chilling and the men were concluding their game of dominoes, I said, "Why is my heart always being broken?"

I'm not sure I was looking for a response, it was more of an expression of how I was feeling. I felt that I was always reaching out to help others, but that when it was my turn to receive help, there was no one around (whether this was true or not, it was how I was feeling at that moment). No sooner had I expressed how I was feeling that the assistant pastor responded with these words: "Your heart is always being broken because you're called to heal the broken-hearted." His words have stuck with me from all those years ago, and I believe that was the Holy Spirit showing me that it was part of my calling.

Can I keep it real? There have been many times in my Christian walk when I have felt like that, and do you know what? Every time that spirit of self-pity or heaviness wants me to engage, I am reminded all the way back to the nineties when that one word, that I was called to heal the broken-hearted, changed everything. Whenever I make the mistake of making it about me, the Lord says, *"Don't take it personally, remember, it's about the people you have been called to serve."* One encounter with the Holy Spirit changes everything!

A church warden's hug

I have worked as a management consultant and coach for many years and observed a gradual shift in the corporate landscape towards being less tolerant of Christianity, even though most organisations have equality, diversity and inclusion policies. More organisations are making their policies restrictive so that sharing faith is no longer acceptable within the workplace.

I'm sharing this to set the scene for an encounter that I will never forget. I was delivering a leadership training session for an organisation and as part of the programme I introduced some diagnostic questionnaires to help the participants grow in their self-awareness. As I began to explain what each element meant and to give real-life examples of how each behaviour plays out in the workplace, one of the participants started to cry. I asked the group to reflect on the lessons they had learned so far and took her outside the room.

As she continued to cry, I felt the Holy Spirit urging me to give her a hug. Hesitating, I reminded the Holy Spirit that I was in a place of work, and it didn't feel appropriate. Then He dropped the 'bomb shell': He said pray for her. "Whatttt?" Here I was, acutely aware of the temperature of the organisation in relation to speaking about faith, standing in front of this short professional English lady who is crying and needing to be consoled, and the Holy Spirit is telling me to pray? I became embroiled in an internal debate. I reminded the Holy Spirit that I needed this contract before doing what I always eventually do: I succumbed to His leading. Let me pause a moment before I continue…

I do question (even though I know through Scripture), why I, and we, debate with the Lord. HE IS GOD and whilst we know this, the flesh is always at war with the Spirit, trying to dominate and get its own way (Galatians 5:16-18). *Father, forgive us again, again in Jesus' name.*

So back to standing outside that door contemplating offering this lady a hug and prayer. She consented to the hug, and then I said, "I know this isn't conventional, but can I pray for you?" At this point, she started to cry even more uncontrollably while nodding her head in agreement at the same time. I cannot remember what I prayed, but as I did, she calmed down. She then shared that she was a church warden at an Anglican church and was feeling lost and that God wasn't hearing her prayers. She had been considering whether she should leave her post. That morning, she had prayed, "God, will you send someone to help me?" Through the training, she had become overwhelmed as the clarity she needed came. Then, to top it off, when I asked if I could pray, she knew it could only be God. She was ecstatic, radiant and peaceful as we returned to the training room. I was just as excited and in awe of God as she was over what He had just done. I had followed His lead and, as always, He didn't let me miss it.

In the natural, everything looked unconventional—hugging a stranger on a training course and praying in the corridors of a public sector workplace. Yet that was where God ordained His breakthrough for His daughter. Can I say it again? In fact, can I shout it from the rooftops:

ONE ENCOUNTER WITH THE HOLY SPIRIT CHANGES THINGS!

Shut it down

I have told the following story many times because it serves as a powerful illustration of how the Holy Spirit has guided me over the years. It was April 2011, and I had been ministering for about

14 years. I had reached a place where I was tired, fed up and frustrated. Although I vehemently believed that God had called me to minister wholeness, purpose and identity to people, it felt like an uphill battle. It was as if I had to peddle the benefits of living a life of wholeness. I was tired and heavily investing my earnings into the ministry to pay for venues and conferencing, and it seemed the returns were few.

We had (and still have) an amazing team of volunteers who pray, lead hospitality, and minister to people who need prayer during our events. One Saturday morning, during our team prayer meeting, I spurted out, "I'm done, let's shut it down." I was convinced that it was time to shut it down—not my relationship with God, but the ministry we were running. On hearing of my decision, the team began to pray for me.

I had a three-day personal retreat booked for myself coming up after that. Before I left, I literally said, "If I don't hear from You, God, I'm done. I'll serve You because You have proved Yourself to be faithful, but no longer will I serve Your people." I do not know if you understand when I say that my mind was made up and I was done, yet at the same time, I wanted peace and whatever God had for my life.

Well, I went to my personal retreat and on the day that I arrived they were hosting a women's onference downstairs. Initially, I had no intention of attending, however, after going to my room, I felt a drawing to go down and sit in the meeting for a while.

As I sat down, the speaker began to speak from Isaiah 61:1-3:

> *"The Spirit of the Sovereign Lord is on me,*
> *because the Lord has anointed me*
> *to proclaim good news to the poor.*

He has sent me to bind up the broken-hearted,
to proclaim freedom for the captives
and release from darkness for the prisoners,
to proclaim the year of the Lord's favour
and the day of vengeance of our God,
to comfort all who mourn,
and provide for those who grieve in Zion—
to bestow on them a crown of beauty
instead of ashes,
the oil of joy
instead of mourning,
and a garment of praise
instead of a spirit of despair.
They will be called oaks of righteousness,
a planting of the Lord
for the display of his splendour."

My ears pricked up because the Scripture the Lord had given me several years before was Luke 4:18-19:

"The Spirit of the Lord is on me,
because he has anointed me
to proclaim good news to the poor.
He has sent me to proclaim freedom for the prisoners
and recovery of sight for the blind,
to set the oppressed free,
to proclaim the year of the Lord's favour."

The Scripture aligned with the words that the pastor had shared with me, that my heart was always being broken because God had a call on my life to heal the broken-hearted. For a season after that encounter, everywhere I went, the Holy Spirit had kept reaffirming these words. Over time He had given me two verses from Scripture in addition to Luke 4:18-19, which are Jeremiah

1:5 and Psalm 139. Whenever I heard one of these three verses, I knew the Lord was speaking to me. He hadn't only spoken to me through His word, but others had also said things or brought the same Scriptures to me in ways that aligned with His word to me. Right up to this day, they remain deeply personal and key to the vision and mission for my life.

When I heard the speaker mention Isaiah 61 at this event, I thought, well, if he had read from Luke 4:18-19, then God may have been speaking to me, but since he hadn't, I had reason to stay in my "I'm ready to shut it down" stance.

Then, as the speaker continued, he said, "Let's turn our Bibles to Luke 4:18-19." Whatever he said after that, I do not recall. God now had my full attention. I went up to my room and asked God what He wanted of me. What was my reason for existing, my purpose? How did He want to use me for His glory? I reminded God (or He reminded me) of the chorus by Milton Brunson, which I had sung on the day of my baptism—"Lord, I'm available to you". The song was like a prayer, as it encapsulated my heart, which was to give my all to God and for Him to use me because I was and, I still am, available to Him.

I went to bed and the following day, I had such a sense of lightness as God clarified my mandate. That day, the word wholeness took on new meaning for me. I knew I wasn't to shut down the ministry but to shut down some of what we were doing and begin to focus on the mandate of wholeness. In those few days, the concept for a series of programmes was developed, and the Wholeness Academy was birthed to teach people about wholeness through Christ Jesus. JPIM were hosting a breakfast in New York that same month, and it was while I was on the aeroplane that I structured the content and programmes.

Why am I telling you all of this? Because one encounter with the Holy Spirit changes everything. From being ready to give up to having a clear mandate to move forward, it could only have been a divine intervention from God.

4

One Encounter with the Holy Spirit Leads to a Breakthrough

t is surprising how a single moment, guided by the divine move of the Holy Spirit, can lead to powerful breakthroughs, often in ways we least expect. Often, a person isn't even aware of the depths of their need until they experience the supernatural intervention of the Holy Spirit. Others may have prayed for an answer to a need or desire for many years. Having spent many years in training and teaching, both as a career and in ministry, I have had the honour of seeing the transformation of numerous lives through God's intervention. Many of these instances happened during the season when I wanted to shut down the ministry. If I were to write about them all, it would be another book, but allow me to share a few that stand out.

Forgiveness for a mother

One person who stands out as an example is Amanda (not her real name). She was invited to one of our conferences by one of our leaders and, despite being sceptical of the Pentecostal style of worship, she felt there was something different about what we were doing. She signed up to attend the Wholeness

Academy, still uncertain, yet feeling a pull to the ministry. During a taught session on forgiveness, Amanda became very resistant to the questions she was being asked about who she had to forgive. She began to share some of the obvious people in her life, but when the Holy Spirit led me to ask her about a particular person, she broke. The Holy Spirit had put His finger on her pain and would not allow her to just go through the motions. He wanted her to address a situation that had been deeply buried.

Do you know, there was a shift in her afterwards that was life-changing. She appeared lighter and more joyful. Amanda has publicly testified on multiple occasions about her uncertainty about the ministry, wondering whether we were legit, but that day, after her encounter with Jesus in that room, everything changed.

That one encounter led to her breakthrough.

But it didn't end there. Amanda also realised she had been holding onto her son, not allowing him to fully flourish. During the session, she was able to forgive herself, and her son was able to forgive her. As a result, their relationship was given the freedom it needed and both have publicly testified about how the Holy Spirit transformed their relationship. One encounter with God changes more than just the individual, it also transforms their families and destinies in other spheres of life. Praise the Lord!

Falling in love with Jesus

Another impactful encounter at the Wholeness Academy that I will always remember is how the Holy Spirit was able to speak directly to the heart of a young man without any of us realising until the end. I was facilitating our Living in Wholeness Programme where several participants experienced breakthroughs. It isn't unusual during these sessions to encounter blocks and obstacles to the participants receiving their breakthrough, that's why prayer and fasting are key: we have no idea what people are carrying when they walk through the door. The very nature of a ministry of wholeness means deliverance and healing will be necessary as we support individuals in their journey.

One of the men on the course seemed to be saying all the right things and to be following along, yet I sensed we were not making headway. So, I paused the session so we could allow the Holy Spirit to intervene. Before I knew it, the song "Falling in love with Jesus", by Jonathan Butler, began to resound in my spirit. I began to gently sing it over the young man as I was led, and he began to break. Later we learned why: it was the song God had used to bring him to the Lord.

As you can imagine, with that blockage out of the way, the Holy Spirit was able to minister to him, and the whole group left the session in awe of that one encounter. Who would know that song would have such meaning to him but the Holy Spirit? Who would know that it wasn't the training materials, the exercises, discussions or ministry that would soften a heart? Only the Holy Spirit. One encounter with the Holy Spirit led to his breakthrough.

Church elder speaks in tongues

I was invited to speak at a church's midweek service where the theme revolved around healing damaged relationships. As I was teaching, my attention was drawn to a warm-looking Caribbean father in the audience, about in his late sixties or early seventies. After I had finished teaching, I invited those who needed reconciliation for a damaged relationship to come forward for prayer. The Holy Spirit moved powerfully among the people and ministered to them in ways only He can.

At the end, the pastor asked if anyone had anything to share and many members spoke about how touched they were and how they received God's healing and blessing.

Then the older gentleman stood up to speak, his face glistening with joy. He just seemed like he was "the cat that got the cream", as the saying goes. He shared that he had always wanted to speak in tongues, but no matter how many times he had been prayed for, he just could not seem to get it. Yet, during my teaching, he felt something rising up in his belly and he began to speak in tongues. He was ecstatic. Now this gentleman was up in age but that day he was like a kid in a sweetshop.

I love it when the Holy Spirit just moves as He will. While healing was taking place, He was also filling his son with a gift he had desired for a long time. ONE ENCOUNTER WITH THE HOLY SPIRIT LED TO A BREAKTHROUGH!

I know that not everyone believes that speaking in tongues is for today's church and that is okay. In my experience, speaking in tongues has led to revelations and opportunities that I could quite easily have missed if I had prayed in the natural.

I was speaking Luganda

Apostle Ruth Kirabo, one of my spiritual daughters, runs a ministry in the UK and Uganda. God has used her to open doors for JPIM to serve in Uganda through the provision of necessary resources to orphans, children and widows, as well as preaching, teaching and ministry to leaders and women. These events are always powerful and life-changing experiences for all who participate. As usual, everything about our trip in October 2022 was orchestrated by the Holy Spirit—but this time it came with an extra Holy Spirit-orchestrated twist. Unlike previous trips that involved several months of preparing, fasting and getting ready, this time, my sister (Rev. Yvonne Atkinson) and I booked our tickets in September, one month before we were on our way in October.

There were moments when we were uncertain we would get there—such as the morning I went to my GP to check my vaccinations were up to date and the nurse told me that there had been an Ebola outbreak in the region we were visiting. The UK government recommended emergency travel only, yet the Holy Spirit gave us peace and the all-clear to move ahead with the mission.

The mission was truly an assignment from the Lord. At the end, Apostle Ruth summed it up well. She said that although we stayed just a week it felt like a month, due to its impact.

We knew the mission had been a success because the attacks we faced during and after were relentless. I fell sick while I was there. One of my worst days was on the Saturday before we returned. Right in the middle of ministering at a conference, I had to run off the stage to go to the bathroom (well, a pit toilet down a hill to be precise). You should have seen the looks on the congregants' faces. Yet, one thing I was determined to do was complete my assignment, and we did. Just a note here: no assignment is completed by one person; there is always a team working together to make things happen. I am thankful for the team of JPIM leaders and volunteers who pray and serve. I am also thankful to a group of Global Intercessors who pray for me and the assignments God leads me to. There is power in prayer.

In preparing for Uganda, I was so fully persuaded that its timing was of God, that if I had to go alone, I was ready to do so. But God… He knew what I would need on that trip and it was a family's love and support back home, and my sister, Rev. Yvonne Atkinson, by my side. While I was sick, I could hear her praying for me as I drifted in and out of sleep and made numerous trips to the bathroom. Thank You, Holy Spirit, for speaking to the people You have put in my life to stand and serve with me.

About a week after arriving back home, I had a dream about Apostle Ruth. In the dream, I was responding to something that was happening, speaking to her with force and saying something like, *"Guh olumba, guh olumba."* When I woke up, I tried to find the meaning of the words, but I had no joy. So, I called her and explained the dream and immediately she told me that it meant, "go and attack". God was giving her a strategy: in this season, you must "go and attack". It wasn't the time to be on the defence, but time to go on the attack.

I had learned a few words and phrases in Luganda so I could connect with the people, however, I had no idea that in my dream, I was speaking Luganda. God wanted to give Apostle Ruth a strategy that we would both know could not be from man. That strategy was indeed a word of direction from the Holy Spirit, bypassing our human logic.

One encounter with the Holy Spirit led to a breakthrough.

A Pastor's Request – "Please lead me to Christ"

I have shared many instances of how the Holy Spirit has shown up in my personal, professional and ministry life. I would like to end with one more encounter that, whilst brief, holds a very special place in my heart.

While on another mission to Uganda some years earlier, I was delivering leadership training at a pastors' and leaders' conference. After I had finished teaching and ministering, one of the interpreters said one of the pastors wanted to speak with me. This pastor had also attended a women's conference I had spoken at prior to the event. They brought her over and she knelt before me as I sat down. The pastor spoke in a local dialect and the interpreter looked surprised as she listened and readied herself to interpret her words.

This pastor had asked the interpreter to ask me if I would lead her to Christ. I was puzzled, thinking there must be a language barrier because she was a pastor herself. Yet that was exactly what she wanted; she wanted Jesus. The pastor explained that, after everything she had heard during the women's conference and now the leadership training and preaching event, she realised that she didn't truly know the Jesus I was teaching about, and she wanted to know Him. I was moved. There and then I led her to Christ and the joy that lit up her face is something I will always remember!

WOW!!!

Did you hear that? A pastor—who I later heard was the overseer of several churches—was humble enough to recognise she needed to know Jesus. She didn't let pride or fear or titles hinder her from pressing in for more, and I, too, was humbled. The Holy Spirit was at work, making Jesus famous.

We, like this dear pastor, can become complacent. Yet that one encounter with the Holy Spirit at a leaders' training day and conference led to a breakthrough that changed everything for this pastor, her congregations and all of us who witnessed it.

I pray that as you have been reading through this section, your heart has been stirred, and you too are crying out to the Lord to know Him—to truly know Him, not just for an encounter, but to be in daily fellowship and union with Him.

This may be a good time to pause and pray:

- Ask God to forgive you for all the times you have overlooked, overrode or dismissed His Spirit's leading. Let the Lord know you are sorry.

- Ask the Holy Spirit to guide you into all truth, and be ready to obey.

- Thank God for His Holy Spirit and pray as you are led in this very moment.

SECTION THREE

The Holy Spirit – Who is He?

5

Who is the Holy Spirit?

As you read through the Scriptures, from Genesis to Revelation, you will encounter the Holy Spirit and His impact. There is also a plethora of literature available that answers the question of who the Holy Spirit is, from personal encounters to the theology of the Holy Spirit, known as pneumatology. My aim in writing this section is to portray what Scripture says about who the Holy Spirit is, presenting attributes and qualities that you will be able to relate to as we prepare to meet Him as Heaven's Sherpa. You will notice overlaps as I endeavour to answer the question posed by this section; I hope this will serve as confirmation, rather than just repetition of what is said.

So, let us begin...

He is God

In Acts 5:1-2, we read of an interaction between a husband and wife, called Ananias and Sapphira. The Holy Spirit had been using the Apostles mightily and the church was growing. The writer tells us that the people lacked nothing because those with land were selling what they had and bringing the money to lay at the feet of the Apostles. Ananias and Sapphira wanted to be a part of what was happening and so sold their property, but then between them agreed to keep some money from the sale for themselves. They then brought the rest of the money to the Apostles.

Peter confronted Ananias and his wife because they presented the money as if it were the full sale amount. In Acts 5:3, he says, *"Ananias, how is it that Satan has so filled your heart that you have lied to the Holy Spirit and have kept for yourself some of the money you received for the land?"* In verse 4, he goes on to say, *"you have not lied to men, but God"*.

Now, let's look at this carefully. In verse 3, Peter says Ananias has lied to the Holy Spirit, and in verse 4, he describes the Holy Spirit as God. So, who is the Holy Spirit? He is God.

I often wonder why Ananias and Sapphira didn't just explain that they had brought some of the proceeds from the sale of our house, instead of allowing Satan to enter their hearts with pride and deceit. As Peter rightly said, the property was theirs, and the proceeds were theirs, so there was really no need to lie. Alas, Ananias and Sapphira paid a hefty price for this lie and died immediately.

How else do we know that the Holy Spirit is God?

The Holy Spirit is Omnipresent

Omnipresence refers to the attribute of being present everywhere at the same time. The term "omnipresence" comes from two Latin words: "omni", meaning all or everywhere, and "presence", meaning existence or being present. It means that

God isn't limited by time, space, or physical boundaries. He is present in all places simultaneously.

Psalm 139:7-8 says, "*Where can I go from your Spirit? Where can I flee from your presence? If I go up to the heavens, you are there; if I make my bed in the depths, you are there.*"

Only God can be here and there, fully present all at the same time. Only God can be in Brooklyn, London, Brazil, Uganda and China, simultaneously. Humans cannot do that, and neither can the devil, however, if you listen to us as Christians at times, you would think Satan possesses omnipresence too. No matter where you travel around the world, you will often hear people say, "The devil is a liar," or "The devil tried to take me out," and the like. He cannot be everywhere at the same time because, like humans, he is a created being. He isn't omnipresent, but God is. The Holy Spirit is omnipresent.

The Holy Spirit is Omniscient

Omniscient describes the attribute of having complete and unlimited knowledge or awareness of all things, including past, present, and future events. It is a term that relates to the nature of God, meaning that He possesses perfect knowledge and understanding of everything that has happened, is happening, and will ever happen in the universe.

So, God, the Holy Spirit is all-knowing, which means He knows all things. Right now, as you read this book, the Holy Spirit is with you (omnipresent). He knows what you are thinking, and He knew what you were thinking this morning. He knows what you will be thinking tomorrow at two o'clock. He knows all things because He is omniscient.

In 1 Corinthians 2:10-11, we read, *"these are the things God has revealed to us by his Spirit. The Spirit searches all things, even the deep things of God. For who knows a person's thoughts except their own spirit within them? In the same way, no one knows the thoughts of God except the Spirit of God."*

In this passage, Paul compares the human spirit to the Spirit of God, signifying that the Holy Spirit possesses divine knowledge and understanding, just as God does. This, again, confirms that the Holy Spirit is God.

The Holy Spirit is Omnipotent

Omnipotent means all-powerfulness or having unlimited power. The Holy Spirit is God and, therefore, carries all the attributes of God the Father and Jesus, including His omnipresence, omniscience and omnipotence.

Luke 1:35 says, *"The angel answered, 'The Holy Spirit will come on you, and the power of the Most High will overshadow you. So the holy one to be born will be called the Son of God.'"*

In this verse, the Holy Spirit is referred to as the source of divine power, playing a crucial role in the miraculous conception of Jesus Christ, our Lord and Saviour.

In another verse, the Apostle Paul attributes the signs and wonders performed during his ministry to the power of the Holy Spirit, underscoring the Spirit's omnipotence in enabling miraculous acts. Romans 15:19 says, *"by the power of signs and wonders, through the power of the Spirit of God. So, from Jerusalem all the way around to Illyricum, I have fully proclaimed the gospel of Christ."*

Jesus promises his disciples that they will receive power from the Holy Spirit, enabling them to boldly spread the message of the Gospel and bear witness to his teachings and promises across the world: *"But you will receive power when the Holy Spirit comes on you, and you will be my witnesses in Jerusalem, and in all Judea and Samaria, and to the ends of the earth."* (Acts 1:8)

Matthew 28:19 is often referred to as the Great Commission. Jesus instructs his disciples, saying, *"Therefore go and make disciples of all nations, baptizing them in the name of the Father and of the Son and of the Holy Spirit."* This verse indicates that the Holy Spirit shares in the same divine authority and nature as the Father and the Son, confirming that the Holy Spirit is God.

Experiencing the Holy Spirit as God

I want to pause here to share a testimony of a personal experience of the Holy Spirit as God that forever changed my family and me. It happened back in 2001, while I was in America, when I received a call from my mum and sister informing me that my dad had gone into hospital with diabetes. His blood sugar had gone so high the doctors could not get a reading. While he was in the hospital, my dad also had a mini heart attack and stroke. I had to ask my mum for the specific details to share it with you because what remains vivid in my memory about that time is first, the shock and fear that struck me because I was so far away that I felt helpless, and secondly, experiencing the Holy Spirit's omnipresence, omniscience and omnipotence all at the same time.

As you can imagine, my first inclination was to immediately get on a plane back to the UK and be with my dad. However, instead of pursuing that route, I felt such an authority rise up within me and the words, "wrong address, return to sender" flowed out of my mouth. I knew it was the Holy Spirit interceding, letting me know this assignment, this illness had arrived at the wrong address and needed to be returned to the depths of hell from where it came. We began praying and every time I heard a report that didn't line up with what we were believing for, I repeated the mantra and confession: "wrong address return to sender". God knew what we needed to ride out that storm because He is omniscient (all-knowing) and we remained steadfast throughout with Him.

I was thousands of miles away yet the same Holy Spirit that was giving me the strategy, authority and boldness to pray was the same Holy Spirit in London, stewarding my dad's healing and comforting my mum and sister as they supported him. The Holy Spirit is all-powerful, all-knowing and present everywhere, and He clearly demonstrated that. Needless to say, my dad came out of hospital with no signs he'd had a stroke or heart attack and he went on to live a fulfilling life, even though he received other diagnoses and eventually went home to be with the Lord in 2017. The events of 2001 stretched our faith and we all came out on the other side knowing the Holy Spirit more than before.

The Holy Spirit is a part of the Trinity

We can see through Scripture that the Holy Spirit is God and He is the third person of the Divine Trinity. I John 5:6-7 says, "*And it is the Spirit who bears witness, because the Spirit is truth. For there are three that bear witness in heaven: the Father, the Word and the Holy Spirit; and these three are one.*" (NKJV)

The Holy Spirit is a member of the Trinity—Father, Son and Holy Ghost. They are three persons, one God.

Over the centuries, there have been various attempts to understand the mysteries of the Trinity. Some have fallen into error, such as Tritheism, a heresy that believes in three distinct separate Gods, instead of one God who exists co-equally and co-eternally in three distinct persons: God the Father, God the Son (Jesus Christ), and God the Holy Spirit. There are Christians who believe in Sabellianism, a movement named after a third-century presbyter named Sabellius, who emphasised the oneness of God, as opposed to God's tri-unity. In fact, Sabellius went as far as to say that there are no distinctions between the "persons" of the Godhead—the one God manifests Himself at different times and for different purposes in three different "modes" or "aspects". This means that God is just three aspects—the Father, the Son and the Holy Spirit—three facets as opposed to three persons. An example I have heard used is the example of a man being a dad, a brother and a son at the same time. These are three aspects of one person.

The truth is, God is love (1 John 4:8 & 16) and to see what love looks like in action, we need to see how the three persons in the Trinity interact. This isn't possible if only one person in the Godhead is acting in three different roles at different times. As I said at the beginning, I understand there will be different schools of thought. We can agree to disagree and at the same time continue to make Jesus famous. Selah…

St. Patrick describes the Trinity as a three-leafed clover, having three different distinct parts. Someone else has likened the Trinity to water. Water is ice, but water is also steam—three distinct manifestations of one. The Spirit of God is part of the Trinity, yet none of these attempts to describe Him can adequately grasp the mysteries of God. We are finite humans who too often try to curtail the immenseness of our God into our human understanding.

Can I keep it real?

After studying theology, I wanted to run away from ministry. The intimate real relationship I had experienced with God up to the point of studying theology was real, simple, unencumbered and pure. Then, as I began studying the history, doctrines and theology of Scripture, it discouraged me, instead of encouraging me. Navigating through the various nuances and beliefs was overwhelming. I often wonder what God thinks of what we have done with His Word. I have no doubt that there are some areas He is well pleased with, but I am also sure there are others that have become more about human comprehension and knowledge than about reaching the lost with the Gospel.

To the human mind, and outside the limits of creation, the Trinity can seem confusing, but God is infinite, possessing all possibility, and beyond our comprehension. To quote R.C. Sproul, "...the doctrine of the Trinity is not a contradiction but a mystery, for we cannot fully understand how God can exist in three Persons, and yet He does."

So, who is the Holy Spirit? HE IS GOD, omnipotent, omnipresent, omniscient, the third person in the holy Trinity, alongside God the Father and God the Son, Jesus.

6

Why Did the Holy Spirit Come?

He was always here...

So often we speak of the coming of the Holy Spirit, relating to the day of Pentecost in the New Testament only, yet He is talked of throughout the Bible, including the Old Testament. In fact, He was there at creation, hovering over the earth as written in Genesis:

Genesis 1:1-2: *"In the beginning, God created the heavens and the earth. The earth was without form, and void; and darkness was on the face of the deep. And the Spirit of God was hovering over the face of the waters."* (NKJV)

Other Scriptures that speak of the Holy Spirit's presence throughout the Bible, including the Old Testament, are:

Isaiah 63:11: *"Then his people recalled the days of old, the days of Moses and his people—where is he who brought them through the sea, with the shepherd of his flock? Where is he who set his Holy Spirit among them..."*

Daniel 5:11: *"There is a man in your kingdom who has the spirit of the holy gods in him. In the time of your father, he was found to have insight and intelligence and wisdom like that of the gods. Your father, King Nebuchadnezzar, appointed him chief of the magicians, enchanters, astrologers and diviners."*

In Section Five, we will also look at examples of how the Holy Spirit moved in the lives of some of those in the Bible and today.

Now that we have set the precedence that the Holy Spirit always was, let us look at why He came. In doing so, we will notice that the reason He came is linked to who He is...

1. He came to represent God on Earth

After Jesus' ascension, the Holy Spirit came to Earth to finish the mission of Christ that commenced in the Gospels and represents God by revealing and glorifying the Father and the Son, empowering us as believers, and uniting us with God. Throughout the Bible, we can see how the Holy Spirit plays a key role in manifesting the Divine Trinity's presence and work among humanity, and He does this through revealing God. John 16:13-15 says, *"But when he, the Spirit of truth, comes, he will guide you into all the truth. He will not speak on his own; he will speak only what he hears, and he will tell you what is yet to come. He will glorify me because it is from me that he will receive what he will make known to you. All that belongs to the Father is mine. That is why I said the Spirit will receive from me what he will make known to you."*

The Holy Spirit is the Spirit of Truth who reveals God's truth to believers. He does not speak independently but communicates what He hears from the Father and the Son. The Holy Spirit's role is to glorify Jesus Christ, highlighting the unity and cooperation within the Trinity. In other words, He is Heaven's representative, representing Heaven here on Earth.

2. He came to glorify Jesus

John 16:14-15 says, *"He will glorify Me, for He will take of what is Mine and declare it to you. All things that the Father has are Mine. Therefore, I said that He will take of Mine and declare it to you."* (NKJV)

This text explicitly notes that the Holy Spirit will glorify Jesus. He glorifies Jesus by focusing attention on Him. He testifies about Jesus (John 15:26) and reveals what He taught us, enabling us to understand and apply God's Word to our lives. The Holy Spirit illuminates the truths of Scripture, bringing us into a deeper relationship with Jesus and leading us to worship and honour Him, in spirit and in truth (John 4:24).

Through the work of the Holy Spirit, we can know Jesus personally, experiencing God's love and grace, as we are empowered to be witnesses and ambassadors for Christ in the world.

3. He came to be a helper to those who believe

John 14:16 says, *"And I will ask the Father, and he will give you another advocate to help you and be with you forever."* In this verse, Jesus is speaking to His disciples, assuring them that after His departure, the Father would send them another Advocate or Helper, which is the Holy Spirit.

The Holy Spirit came to help believers by convicting people of their sin, righteousness, and judgment (John 16:8), guiding them toward a righteous and God-honouring life.

The Holy Spirit also helps us by providing comfort and consolation, especially in times of difficulty, sorrow, or uncertainty (2 Corinthians 1:3-4). In His role as Comforter, He also offers the peace of God that surpasses all understanding (Philippians 4:7), reassuring us of God's love and presence.

The Holy Spirit also helps by equipping believers for effective Christian living and service. Through the gifts and empowerment of the Holy Spirit, believers receive the tools necessary to carry out God's purposes in the world (1 Corinthians 12:4-11).

We also explore the Holy Spirit as our helper in the next section on the names of the Holy Spirit.

4. He came to be a guide

John 16:13 says, *"But when he, the Spirit of truth, comes, he will guide you into all the truth. He will not speak on his own; he will speak only what he hears, and he will tell you what is yet to come."*

Here, Jesus speaks to His disciples about the Holy Spirit's future ministry. The Spirit of Truth guides believers into all truth, revealing God's divine wisdom and deep treasure of the Word. As a guide, the Holy Spirit leads and directs us as believers in our walk with God. He is instrumental in helping us to understand God's will, navigate life's challenges, and grow in our relationship with Him.

Romans 8:14 says, *"For those who are led by the Spirit of God are the children of God."* The Scripture emphasises that the Holy Spirit leads those who belong to God, signifying the Spirit's guiding presence in the lives of believers. We are also implored to walk by the Spirit, which means being guided by the Holy Spirit's promptings and direction, leading to a life aligned with

God's will and free from the desires of the flesh. *"So, I say, walk by the Spirit, and you will not gratify the desires of the flesh."* (Galatians 5:16)

The Holy Spirit will speak to you about what is going on and things to come. Those little impressions we feel when we say, "I felt like going this way." It wasn't that *you* felt to go that way, it is the Holy Spirit communicating that there may be an obstacle ahead of you or that you need to go a different way because there is someone you need to meet, and more. As I said earlier, enough of luck, happenstance, feelings, coincidence and the like getting the praise for what the Holy Spirit has orchestrated.

As we yield to the Holy Spirit's guidance, we can experience God's transformative work in our lives, aligning our actions, thoughts, and decisions with His perfect will. The Holy Spirit's guidance enables us to live in obedience to God and experience the abundant life that comes from walking with Him (John 10:10).

5. He came to bring truth

John 14:16-17 says, *"And I will ask the Father, and he will give you another advocate to help you and be with you forever—the Spirit of truth. The world cannot accept him because it neither sees him nor knows him. But you know him, for he lives with you and will be in you."*

Another reason the Holy Spirit came is to bring truth. As we have seen, He is often referred to as the Spirit of Truth, who dwells within believers and guides them into the knowledge and understanding of God's Word. Throughout the Bible, the Holy Spirit is depicted as the One who unfolds the Scriptures, guiding believers into a deeper understanding of its teachings and reminding them of what Jesus Christ taught. There are always deeper revelations to be gleaned from Scripture, but the Holy Spirit ensures that our interpretations are biblical.

Earlier we read John 16:13, which says, *"But when he, the Spirit of truth, comes, he will guide you into all truth. He will not speak on his own; he will speak only what he hears, and he will tell you what is yet to come."* In this capacity, the Holy Spirit guides believers into all truth, not by speaking independently but by conveying what He receives from the Father and the Son. The Spirit reveals future truths to us (such as through prophecy or word of knowledge), enabling us to comprehend the things of God, including His redemptive plan. The Holy Spirit came to testify about Jesus Christ, so we can grow in the knowledge of God's Word and will, empowering us to live in alignment with the truth and experience the freedom and transformation that comes from doing so.

6. He convicts us of sin

John 16:8–11, says, *"And when He has come, He will convict the world of sin, and of righteousness, and of judgment: of sin, because they do not believe in Me; of righteousness, because I go to My Father and you see Me no more; of judgment, because the ruler of this world is judged."* (NKJV)

The Holy Spirit came to convict us of sin. This conviction is a crucial part of the Spirit's work in the lives of individuals, leading them to acknowledge their need for God's forgiveness and transforming power. The conviction of sin is a loving act of the Holy Spirit, drawing people to repentance and reconciliation with God.

I'm reminded of King David's prayer in Psalm 51:10: *"Create in me a pure heart, O God, and renew a steadfast spirit within me."*

This was a prayer of repentance, revealing how the Holy Spirit convicted David of his sin with Bathsheba (full story in 2 Samuel 11–12:25). The Spirit's conviction led him to seek God's forgiveness, and it is the same with us. So many people see God as some big angry force in Heaven, but the fact that He sent His Holy Spirit to help us back to Him is yet another demonstration of His incredible and unfailing love towards us. I am thankful, and hope you are too.

The conviction of the Holy Spirit serves as a catalyst for people to recognise their need for God's grace and salvation. It leads to repentance and turning away from sin, allowing us to experience God's forgiveness and the transformative power of the Holy Spirit. The Holy Spirit's work of conviction is a manifestation of God's loving and redeeming nature, drawing people closer to Him and bringing them into a renewed and restored relationship with our Heavenly Father.

7. He came for us to receive power

Acts 1:8 instructs us that, *"When the Holy Spirit has come upon you, you will receive power and will tell people about me everywhere—in Jerusalem, throughout Judea, in Samaria and to the ends of the earth."* Jesus promises the disciples that they will receive power when the Holy Spirit comes upon them. This power enables them to be effective witnesses; it describes the courage and willingness we need to spread the Gospel of the Kingdom of God.

I believe this is one of the Holy Spirit's significant purposes and an area where we need to press in more as the body of Christ. We live in a world where unbelief is rife and we need the power of the Holy Spirit to begin to break into the darkness that prevails. The Holy Spirit empowers us in so many ways to live according to God's will, carry out our calling, and be effective witnesses for Christ.

Ephesians 3:16 says, "*I pray that out of his glorious riches he may strengthen you with power through his Spirit in your inner being.*" Here, again, Paul's prayer for the Ephesian believers emphasises that the Holy Spirit strengthens them with divine power internally. This power enables believers to grow spiritually, resist temptation, and bear spiritual fruit. Paul also prayed for believers in Romans 15:13 to experience the power of the Holy Spirit, leading to an overflow of hope, joy, and peace. Finally, Galatians 5:16 says, "*So I say, walk by the Spirit, and you will not gratify the desires of the flesh.*" The Holy Spirit's indwelling presence provides believers with the power to resist the desires of the flesh and live in obedience to God.

The power of the Holy Spirit isn't limited to external manifestations but also includes inner strength, wisdom, and boldness to live according to God's Word and to fulfil His calling. The Holy Spirit's power equips us to face challenges, overcome obstacles, and bear witness to the love and truth of Jesus Christ in our lives. When we learn to rely on the power of the Holy Spirit, we experience the transformative work of God, enabling us to live in alignment with God's purposes and to glorify Him in all we do.

8. He came to help us be a witness

Acts 1:8 tells us, "*When the Holy Spirit has come upon you, you will receive power and will tell people about me everywhere—in Jerusalem, throughout Judea, in Samaria and to the ends of the earth.*"

Before Jesus' ascension, He promises the disciples that they will receive power when the Holy Spirit comes upon them. This power enables them to be witnesses, sharing the message of the good news of salvation to the ends of the earth. The Holy Spirit came to be a witness, testifying about Jesus Christ and empowering believers to be witnesses of His life, death, and resurrection. The point here is being empowered to know *what to say.*

Acts 5:32 says, *"We are witnesses of these things, and so is the Holy Spirit, whom God has given to those who obey him."*

The Apostles declare that they are witnesses of Jesus' life, death, and resurrection. They, along with the Holy Spirit, testify to the truth of the Gospel. The Holy Spirit empowers believers to be effective witnesses of Jesus Christ, both guiding us in our witness and providing us with the boldness and words to share the Good News with others. The Holy Spirit's testimony isn't only external but also internal, confirming the truth of Christ in our hearts and enabling us to bear witness to His transforming work in our lives. As we yield to the leading of the Holy Spirit, the compounded effect of the various reasons He came transforms us into powerful ambassadors. Everything about us changes (see 1 Samuel 9-11 and Acts 9).

So, why did the Holy Spirit come? The Holy Spirit was always here. He has been spoken of and His presence noted from creation.

On the day of Pentecost, He came as Jesus had promised to be Heaven's Representative on Earth, to testify of and glorify Jesus. He came to help us as believers to be a witness. He came to convict us of our sins, to guide us, endue us with power and bring truth.

7

Titles and Names of the Holy Spirit

The Holy Spirit is the most commonly used name for the third person of the Holy Trinity, as found in Acts 1:8: *"But you will receive power when the Holy Spirit comes on you..."* The title "Holy Spirit" emphasises the divine and pure nature of the Spirit. The word "holy" speaks of perfection, moral purity, and being set apart from all that is sinful and unclean. Yet it isn't the only name found in Scripture for Him. There are many others, too.

The Holy Spirit is also referred to as the **Spirit of God or Spirit of the Lord**. Genesis 1:2, says, *"The Spirit of God was hovering over the waters."* And Luke 3:22 says, *"and the Holy Spirit descended on him in bodily form like a dove. And a voice came from heaven: 'You are my Son, whom I love; with you, I am well pleased.'"*

As the Spirit of God or the Spirit of the Lord, the Holy Spirit is inseparably linked with God the Father and God the Son, because He is holy, as stated above.

The Holy Spirit is also given the title or name **Comforter (Counsellor or Advocate)**. John 14:16 says, *"And I will ask the*

Father, and he will give you another Advocate to help you and be with you forever." The Holy Spirit is called the Comforter because He comes alongside us to console, encourage, and strengthen us.

As the Counsellor, He provides divine guidance, wisdom, and advice. As the Advocate, the Holy Spirit acts as a legal representative, supporting believers and interceding for us before God. The titles highlight the Spirit's intimate and personal involvement in our lives, comforting us in times of need and advocating for our well-being.

I love John 14:17 in the Amplified Translation, which says, *"And I will ask the Father, and He will give you another Helper (Comforter, Advocate, Intercessor—Counsellor, Strengthener, Standby), to be with you forever."* Yes, He is all of that and so much more…

The Holy Spirit is called **Spirit of Truth**. John 16:13 says, *"But when he, the Spirit of truth, comes, he will guide you into all the truth. He will not speak on his own; he will speak only what he hears, and he will tell you what is yet to come."*

The title "Spirit of Truth" points to the Holy Spirit's role in revealing divine truths and guiding us into a deeper understanding of God's will. The Spirit testifies to the truth of Jesus Christ and helps us discern spiritual realities from falsehood. As the Spirit of Truth, He ensures that believers align their lives with God's Word as revealed in Scripture.

He is also called **Spirit of Wisdom and Revelation**. Ephesians 1:17 says, *"I keep asking that the God of our Lord Jesus Christ, the glorious Father, may give you the Spirit of wisdom and revelation, so that you may know him better."*

The verse highlights the role of the Holy Spirit as the source of wisdom and revelation. As believers, we can ask God for wisdom and revelation so that we may know Jesus better through the Holy Spirit, as wisdom and revelation. Before going into a meeting, I will ask God to give me Heaven's strategies for what is about to be discussed. When preparing for the day, I will ask God to give me wisdom for what is ahead, and as I read His Word, I ask for revelation to help me grow—"What do you want to reveal today, Lord?" or "What do you want to show me?" One word of wisdom or revelation can save you years of unnecessary striving.

Another name for the Holy Spirit is **Spirit of Wisdom and Understanding**. Isaiah 11:2 says, "*The Spirit of the Lord will rest on him—the Spirit of wisdom and of understanding, the Spirit of counsel and of might, the Spirit of the knowledge and fear of the Lord.*"

The Holy Spirit is referred to as the Spirit of Wisdom and Understanding because He imparts divine wisdom, insight, and discernment to us. Through the Holy Spirit's influence, we are enlightened and have the ability to gain spiritual insight into God's Word and His purposes. The Spirit's wisdom helps us to make godly decisions and live according to God's will.

He is also referred to as the **Spirit of Adoption**. Romans 8:15 says, "*The Spirit you received does not make you slaves so that you live in fear again; rather, the Spirit you received brought about your adoption to sonship. And by him, we cry, 'Abba, Father.'*"

The Spirit of Adoption highlights the Holy Spirit's role in confirming we are children of God. Through the Holy Spirit's work, we experience a deep sense of belonging in God's family, with all the privileges and inheritance of sons and daughters of the Most High God. The Spirit assures those who believe of their intimate relationship with God, so we are able to cry out "Abba, Father" with affection and trust.

Spirit of Power, Love, and Self-discipline are also titles given to the Holy Spirit. In 2 Timothy 1:7 we read, *"For the Spirit God gave us does not make us timid, but gives us power, love, and self-discipline."*

The Holy Spirit empowers us with spiritual power to overcome challenges, face adversity, and carry out God's purposes. His presence ignites love within us, inspiring us to love God and others genuinely and sacrificially. Additionally, the Spirit empowers believers with self-discipline, enabling us to exercise self-control over our desires and emotions. This is a Scripture many of us as Christians know so well and often quote: *"God has not given me a spirit of fear, but of power and of love and a sound mind."* The truth is, it is one thing to quote what He hasn't given us, but quite another (and far more powerful) to identify with Him who is within us, and that is the Spirit of Power, Love and Self-Discipline.

We also find that the Holy Spirit is called **Spirit of Life**. Romans 8:2 says, *"because through Christ Jesus the law of the Spirit who gives life has set you free from the law of sin and death".* As the Spirit of Life, the Holy Spirit brings spiritual life to believers. Through the Spirit's regenerating work, believers are born again, becoming new creations in Christ (2 Corinthians 5:17). The Holy Spirit liberates believers from the bondage of sin and death, giving us an expectancy and assurance of not only eternal life in Heaven but also a transformed and fruitful life here on Earth in fellowship with God.

He is called **Helper**. John 14:27 (AMP) says, *"But the Helper (Comforter, Advocate, Intercessor—Counsellor, Strengthener, Standby), the Holy Spirit, whom the Father will send in My name [in My place, to represent Me and act on My behalf], He will teach you all things. And He will help you remember everything that I have told you."*

The Greek word "helper" or "advocate" is paraclete, used to describe the Holy Spirit's role alongside believers. John 14:16 says, *"And I will ask the Father, and he will give you another advocate to help you and be with you forever."*

Wow! I know I have already touched on this earlier, however, if we were to truly grasp who we have living on the inside of us and the help that is readily available, we would call upon the Holy Spirit, our Helper, far more readily.

I do not know about you, but as I revisit who the Holy Spirt is, the same Spirit that raised Jesus from the dead, the same Spirit that drew you (and in some cases dragged you) into the Kingdom, the same God that is omnipotent, omnipresent and omniscient, possessing mind, will, emotions and power, I am overwhelmed with gratitude and amazement that He says He is your Helper! *Commmmmeeee oooonnn!* I am excited all over again to decrease that the Spirit might increase in my life, in Jesus' name. For He is our Comforter, Advocate, Intercessor—Counsellor, Strengthener and Standby, hallelujah!

In the Bible, we also find the title **Spirit of Christ** is given to the Holy Spirit. Romans 8:9, *"You, however, are not in the realm of the flesh but are in the realm of the Spirit if indeed the Spirit of God lives in you. And if anyone does not have the Spirit of Christ, they do not belong to Christ."*

This verse highlights the close relationship between the Holy Spirit and Jesus Christ. According to Blue Letter Bible, "The reason why the Holy Spirit is called the 'Spirit of Jesus Christ,' the 'Spirit of Jesus,' and the 'Spirit of His Son' is because He was sent by Jesus to remind the world of what Jesus did – not because they are the same Person." We see this in Jesus' own words in John 14:26. The Holy Spirit is the Spirit of Christ.

These names and titles of the Holy Spirit are not exhaustive, yet they reveal the multi-faceted nature of the Spirit's work in our lives, emphasising His guidance, comfort, wisdom, adoption, empowerment, and more.

Many years ago, I read the book, *Heavenly Man*, the autobiography of a Chinese Christian called Brother Yun, who endured many hardships and persecution for his faith in Christ. I know some people have questioned the accuracy of some details of his testimony, but the relevance of his story lies in its examples of faith, endurance, and the work of the Holy Spirit during adversity. His story is a good example of the multi-faceted nature of the names and titles of the Holy Spirit we have just looked at, as well as the attributes we will look at in the next chapter. Let us look at some of the ways the Holy Spirit worked through Brother Yun's experience.

The Holy Spirit at work

In the darkest moments of his imprisonment, Brother Yun often found himself sustained by the presence of the Holy Spirit and would pray fervently for strength and guidance. There were times when he felt utterly alone and isolated, but in those moments, he would sense the comforting and empowering presence of the Holy Spirit with him. The Spirit would bring to his mind scriptures and promises from the Bible, reminding him of God's faithfulness and giving him the courage to endure.

During one of his imprisonments, Brother Yun faced what looked like a hopeless situation. He had been placed in a small, dark cell where he was isolated and subjected to physical abuse. He felt overwhelmed by despair and was unsure how much longer he could endure. In the midst of his suffering, he cried out to God for strength and guidance.

One day, as he was praying, he experienced a powerful visitation from the Holy Spirit. In his book, Brother Yun describes how the Spirit's presence filled his cell, bringing undeniable and powerful peace and comfort that he had never known before. He felt as if Jesus Himself was standing there with him, radiating love and assurance. In that moment, he was reminded of the promise from Jesus that He would never leave nor forsake His followers.

During this encounter with the Holy Spirit, Brother Yun received a vision of his family and fellow believers who were also enduring persecution. He saw their faces and felt a deep sense of unity and interconnectedness with the global body of Christ. The Spirit spoke to his heart, assuring him that he wasn't alone, and that countless brothers and sisters were standing with him in spirit.

Knowing this filled him with courage and faith and Brother Yun began to sing praises to God within his prison cell, alerting his fellow inmates who were taken aback by his joy and resilience in the face of suffering. This encounter with the Holy Spirit marked a turning point in his imprisonment. He no longer felt alone or defeated, but empowered by the Spirit's presence.

Through this experience, Brother Yun gained a fresh revelation of the Holy Spirit's role as Comforter and Advocate. The Spirit not only provided supernatural comfort in the midst of his suffering but also empowered him to minister to others in the prison. He continued to share the Gospel with fellow inmates and even some of the prison guards, all under the guidance and anointing of the Holy Spirit. There are many other examples of the Holy Spirit guiding Brother Yun through his ministry, including instances when he felt a strong leading to take certain risks or paths that seemed counterintuitive. When he trusted in the Spirit's direction, time and time again, these steps of faith led to miraculous interventions and opportunities to share the love of Christ.

Just as the Holy Spirit showed up in Brother Yun's life, so is He available to make His presence known in our lives. It might not always be in ways as dramatic but He is continuously working things out on our behalf. We can trust Him. As Heaven's Sherpa guides, He reflects the names He is known by, shaping and transforming us while making a way through. We, too, come to know Him as Comforter, Helper, Spirit of Power, Love, and Self-discipline, Spirit of Wisdom and Revelation and so much more, as He works to help us navigate the terrains of life.

My prayer is that as you reflect on the names of the Holy Spirit, they will reveal more and more of who it is you have guiding, comforting and leading you. It is my prayer that you begin to press into Him, speak to Him, cooperate with Him, partner with Him, rely on Him and trust Him. He has access and knowledge to Heaven, along with Heaven's strategies, wisdom, leadership and backing. How powerful!

Having explored who the Holy Spirit is and how He is revealed through some of His names, it's time to delve into His attributes. Again, I pray the next part of our journey will provide a deeper understanding of who the Holy Spirit is, why He came and His role among us as believers.

8

Attributes of the Holy Spirit

A s we transition from exploring the names of the Holy Spirit, we are now going to focus on the heart of His attributes. These facets of His divine nature provide us with a clearer understanding of His character, purpose, and the remarkable ways He turns up in our lives as believers. Just as a precious stone reveals its brilliance from various angles, so does examining the attributes of the Holy Spirit help us understand the depth of His presence and power. Let us now move on in our exploration of Heaven's Sherpa, the Holy Spirit who guides, empowers, and transforms us from within.

He is a person

The Holy Spirit is a person, but not an ordinary person, He is a divine person. I searched through the Scriptures to find where the Holy Spirit was referred to as 'it', but could not find a single reference. I wonder if there has been a misunderstanding as to the Holy Spirit's personhood because of some of the symbols that are used to convey different aspects of His nature and work. One example is wind. In John 3:8, it says, "*The wind blows wherever it pleases. You hear its sound, but you cannot tell where it comes from or where it is going. So, it is with everyone born of the Spirit."*

This text is taken from part of a conversation Jesus was having with Nicodemus (John 3:1-21). Jesus uses the wind as an analogy to explain the mysterious nature of the Holy Spirit's work in our lives. The Spirit's presence and activity can be felt, but His movements are beyond human control or prediction.

Another symbol used to describe the impact of the Holy Spirit's presence is fire. Acts 2:3 says, *"They saw what seemed to be tongues of fire that separated and came to rest on each of them."* On the day of Pentecost, the Holy Spirit descended upon the disciples in the form of a mighty rushing wind and tongues of fire. This event marked the outpouring of the Holy Spirit and the birth of the early Church. The Holy Spirit appeared as tongues of fire, symbolising the Spirit's purifying, empowering, and transformative nature.

Water is another powerful symbol associated with the Holy Spirit in the Bible. Just as wind and fire carry significant spiritual meaning that portrays the various aspects of the Holy Spirit's work in our lives, so does water. John 7:37-39 says, *"On the last and greatest day of the festival, Jesus stood and said in a loud voice, 'Let anyone who is thirsty come to me and drink. Whoever believes in me, as Scripture has said, rivers of living water will flow from within them.' By this, he meant the Spirit, whom those who believed in him were later to receive. Up to that time, the Spirit had not been given since Jesus had not yet been glorified."*

In this passage, Jesus speaks of the Holy Spirit as "rivers of living water" that would flow from within believers. Just as water quenches thirst, refreshes, satisfies and gives life to the human body, the Holy Spirit brings the same in the spirit to all those who believe in Jesus.

Water also symbolises the cleansing nature of the Holy Spirit's new birth: *"Jesus answered, 'Very truly I tell you, no one can enter the kingdom of God unless they are born of water and the Spirit'"* (John 3:5; see also Ezekiel 36:25–27).

These Scriptures illustrate the profound connection between the Holy Spirit and fire, wind and water. Other symbols include a dove (Matthew 3:16-17), wine (Acts 2:15 – 17), oil (Luke 4:18, 1 Samuel 16:13) and a seal or a pledge (2 Corinthians 2:22, Ephesians 1:13-14). These references highlight the Spirit's dynamic and life-changing role in our lives.

Dr. R. A. Torrey, communicating the importance of the personality of the Spirit and of our being, assured us of this fact when he said: "If the Holy Spirit is a Divine Person and we know it not, we are robbing a Divine Being of the love and adoration which are His due. It is of the highest practical importance whether the Holy Spirit is a power that we, in our ignorance and weakness, are somehow to get hold of and use, or whether the Holy Spirit is a personal Being... who is to get hold of us and use us. It is of the highest experimental importance...Many can testify to the blessing that came into their lives when they came to know the Holy Spirit, not merely as gracious influence...but as an ever-present, loving friend and helper." (*The Great Doctrines of the Bible*; Evans; 1981)

He has a mind

In 1 Corinthians 2:10-11, we read, *"These are the things God has revealed to us by his Spirit. The Spirit searches all things, even the deep things of God. For who knows a person's thoughts except their own spirit within them? In the same way, no one knows the thoughts of God except the Spirit of God."*

As I read this text, I see that the Holy Spirit is a thinker. He has thoughts; therefore He has a mind.

When we think about someone having a mind, we think of a person with the capacity to think, reason, perceive, understand, learn, and be conscious of their experiences. The mind is often associated with mental processes such as cognition, emotions, memory, imagination, and consciousness. In humans, the mind is an integral part of the brain's functioning; it is the engine room for our cognitive functions and mental activities. It allows us to process information from the external world, make decisions, form beliefs, solve problems, and engage in creative thinking. The mind plays a crucial role in shaping behaviour, attitudes, and responses to the environment.

There are different philosophical and scientific theories that have attempted to explain the nature of the mind, its functions, and its relationship to the physical body and the external world. It isn't my objective to unpick those here but to acknowledge there are differing theories concerning the mind. My rationale for including this is to help you gain a full picture of the person of the Holy Spirit, so that as you continue on your journey to develop a meaningful relationship with Him, you receive Him, in the fullness of who He is.

For example, there are days when I am in the middle of doing something and I pause to simply say, "What do You think, Holy Spirit?" On occasions, I immediately find the answer to my question and on others, the answer comes later, yet I am fully persuaded that it is the Holy Spirit who responded. For example, while writing this book, I sensed His familiar unction to include a specific example. I was in the middle of another train of thought and instead of making a note to return to it, I assumed I would remember. When it was time to include the additional example, I just could not recall what it was. I repented for overriding His lead and thought it would come straight back to me, but it didn't. Then, as I continued writing, I heard so clearly what it was and, this time, immediately noted it down for inclusion.

I am on His schedule, He isn't on mine; He is Lord, I am not. The sooner that sinks in for all of us, the better.

I remember someone describing the prophetic and dream world as being one painted or written with invisible ink, and I get it. If I fail to intentionally write down my dreams, I forget them. Thankfully, there are times when by His absolute grace while in the middle of a task or speaking to someone, parts of the dream start to unfold.

The Holy Spirit is a divine person with a mind. Selah... Pause and think on this.

He has emotions

As we study the Scriptures, we begin to see that the God of the universe has emotions. God the Father loved (John 3:16), He got angry (Deuteronomy 9:8) and was jealous (Exodus 20:5). Jesus got angry (Matthew 21:12-13), He wept (John 11:35) and He loved (John 14:34). If God the Father and Jesus have emotions, why not the Holy Spirit who is co-equal and co-eternal within the Trinity?

Emotions are a fundamental part of what it means to be human, shaping our experiences and influencing how we perceive and interact with the world. Having emotions refers to the capacity of people to experience and express various feelings and sensations, often in response to internal or external stimuli. Emotions are an integral part of the human experience, shaping how we perceive and interact with the world around us. They encompass a wide range of emotional states, from joy and love to sadness, fear, anger, and more.

Through our emotions, we are able to connect with others, empathise, and understand both theirs and our own needs and desires. Yes, emotions can sometimes be challenging to navigate, but they also add depth and richness to our lives, contributing to our emotional intelligence and overall well-being. It is difficult to imagine what our experience of life would resemble without them. Rather than ignoring or allowing them to run wild, learning to recognise, understand, and manage our emotions can lead to healthier relationships, greater resilience, and a more meaningful and fulfilling life.

I love that the Bible captured some of the emotions that God Himself experienced. The writer of the Book of Hebrews took it a step further when he said in chapter 4, verse 15, *"For we do not have a high priest who is unable to empathize with our weaknesses, but we have one who has been tempted in every way, just as we are—yet he did not sin."* He depicted His full understanding of the range of emotions we as believers would experience on Earth.

The Bible also reveals that the Holy Spirit can be grieved. Ephesians 4:30 says, *"And do not grieve the Holy Spirit of God, with whom you were sealed for the day of redemption."*

This verse implies a personal and emotional aspect of the Holy Spirit's nature, as grief is an emotional response to something that causes sorrow and pain. If you have ever faced resistance while being prompted by the Holy Spirit to act on a direction, whether that resistance originated from inside you or from an outside force, then you will likely have experienced this feeling of heavy discomfort inside.

Again, we see the Holy Spirit can be grieved from Isaiah 63:10, which says, "*Yet they rebelled and grieved his Holy Spirit. So, he turned and became their enemy and he himself fought against them.*"

This Old Testament passage speaks of the Holy Spirit being grieved by the rebellious actions of the people of Israel, that would lead to consequences. As I have already said, we must be under no illusion, the Holy Spirit can be grieved and Ephesians 4:30 clearly instructs us not to do so.

Finally, in Galatians 5:22-23, the Bible says, "*But the fruit of the Spirit is love, joy, peace, forbearance, kindness, goodness, faithfulness, gentleness, and self-control.*"

Here, the "fruit of the Spirit" refers to the attributes that the Holy Spirit produces in our lives. Love, joy, and peace are emotions or emotional states that the Holy Spirit helps to cultivate within us. To cultivate something, one must have it first, so, clearly, the Holy Spirit has emotions.

These Scriptures start to help us to see that the Holy Spirit isn't an impersonal force but rather a divine person with emotions, thoughts, and intentions. The Holy Spirit displays love, joy and grief, among other personal attributes. When we understand the personal nature of the Holy Spirit, it helps us relate to Him in a more intimate and personal way, which in turn enables us to experience the Spirit's presence and work in our lives.

He has a will

The Holy Spirit is a divine person with a will. Remember, He is fully God. He possesses distinct personal attributes, including intellect, emotions, and the will to choose and to act. We read in 1 Corinthians 12:11, *"But one and the same Spirit works all these things, distributing to each one individually as He wills"* (NKJV). The verse speaks of the Holy Spirit's active involvement in distributing spiritual gifts to believers, indicating the Spirit's wilful decisions in carrying out this task.

Having a will refers to the capacity of a person being able to make conscious choices, decisions, and intentions. It is the ability to have desires, preferences, and goals, and to act upon them that enables us to get tasks done, to improve our lives, to apply God-given solutions to the problems we see around us. In essence, having a will is a fundamental part of being human. It enables us to exercise control over our thoughts, actions, and behaviour, and to navigate our lives. Having a will implies that we can deliberate, plan, and set objectives, as well as take responsibility for the consequences of our decisions. It truly is a gift and blessing to us, mirrored in the fact that the Holy Spirit possesses a will as well, as Scripture clearly demonstrates.

He is Holy

The Holy Spirit is inherently holy, and His presence works to sanctify and transform us into the likeness of Christ (1 Peter 1:15-16). This role is significant in the process of changing our lives, enabling us to live the way God intended. Known as sanctification, it refers to the ongoing work of the Holy Spirit in transforming us to become more like Christ, conforming us to God's moral and spiritual standards. The Holy Spirit works within us to produce holy character and conduct, which we could not do for ourselves. It is holiness that sanctifies believers and makes us temples of the living God (1 Corinthians 6:19-20).

The holiness of the Holy Spirit is a fundamental aspect of His nature and character. It sets the Holy Spirit apart as divine and pure, and His sanctification work in the lives of believers includes conviction of sin, empowerment, and spiritual discernment. As the Holy Spirit does this work in our lives, He helps us to grow in holiness and draw closer to God.

He is an Intercessor

Romans 8:26-27 says, "*In the same way, the Spirit helps us in our weakness. We do not know what we ought to pray for, but the Spirit himself intercedes for us through wordless groans. And he who searches our hearts knows the mind of the Spirit, because the Spirit intercedes for God's people in accordance with the will of God.*"

The Spirit also intercedes for believers in prayer, advocating for us before God and expressing our needs, even when we are unable to articulate them ourselves. How incredible! God the Holy Spirit is our Intercessor. Do you know what that means? Do you remember earlier when I spoke about praying Spirit-led prayers? This is in part how we see the Holy Spirit interceding on our behalf. When we are unsure of what to pray, He is right there, interceding for us and others, which means with Holy Spirit-powered prayers, we can never pray amiss. I do not know about you, but that gets me ready to shout, "Hallelujah!!!"

He is Teacher

The Holy Spirit is the ultimate teacher, instructing believers in the ways of God, revealing and illuminating the truths of

Scripture (1 Corinthians 2:13), so that we can be doers, and not just hearers.

In John 14:26, Jesus assures His disciples that the Holy Spirit, whom the Father will send in His name, will teach them all things and remind them of His teachings. This promise is reinforced in John 16:13, where Jesus calls the Holy Spirit the Spirit of Truth, who guides believers into godly knowledge and declares to them the things that are to come.

Reading 1 Corinthians 2:10-12 affirms that God reveals His wisdom and truth through the Spirit, allowing believers to understand the deep things of God. Furthermore, in 1 John 2:27, it is written that the anointing of the Holy Spirit teaches believers about everything and abides in them. The Holy Spirit's role as Teacher is vital in guiding, empowering, and transforming us as we seek to live in alignment with God's will, Word and purpose.

He speaks

The Bible says the Holy Spirit speaks. Acts 8:29 says, *"The Spirit told Philip, 'Go to that chariot and stay near it.'"* Acts 10:19 says, *"While Peter was still thinking about the vision, the Spirit said to him, 'Simon, three men are looking for you.'"* Acts 13:3 says, *"While they were worshiping the Lord and fasting, the Holy Spirit said, 'Set apart for me Barnabas and Saul for the work to which I have called them.'"* 2 Samuel 23:2 says, *"'The Spirit of the Lord spoke through me; his word was on my tongue.'"*

These are just a few instances where Scripture confirms the Holy Spirit speaks. He also speaks by bearing witness in the spirit of believers, confirming our relationship with God and assuring us of our salvation (Romans 8:16).

The Holy Spirit speaks through revelation that helps us understand spiritual truths found in the Bible (1 Corinthians 2:10-12). What does this mean? Have you ever been reading a particular verse in the Bible and suddenly it is illuminated to you, speaking to a situation you are going through right then and there? Or have you ever read a passage of Scripture numerous times before but not fully understood it, and then on a particular day, you read it and it makes sense, coming alive? Sometimes we believe we understand a verse until the Holy Spirit speaks through it and then wham… That's the Holy Spirit within you bringing illumination to God's Word, so you can grasp and apply it to your life.

The Holy Spirit convicts people of their sin, righteousness, and judgment (John 16:8). He prompts a person to recognise and turn away from wrongdoing and turn towards God's righteousness.

The Holy Spirit leads us and guides us in making decisions in accordance with God's will. He provides direction through prompting and leading us in our daily lives (Romans 8:14). The Holy Spirit will speak through prophetic utterances, speaking the heart of God in a situation through words of wisdom, knowledge and prophecy (1 Corinthians 12:7-11). Wow, that is quite a lot!

Some people have testified to hearing the Holy Spirit speak as a still quiet voice. Some people have said they heard an audible voice. Most of us will have experienced the Holy Spirit's voice as inspired ideas and thoughts. This, like every other spiritual leading, should be tested as we know our own human thoughts can be mistaken for the leading of the Holy Spirit (more on this in Section Five). However, you may have been praying about a situation that you need God's guidance for when all of a sudden, an idea comes to you and it is literally a Godsend. That is the Holy Spirit inspiring, guiding, teaching and leading as Jesus said He would (John 14:26).

He reveals our true identity

To conclude this section, I would like to explain why I have taken the time to share this section about the Holy Spirit with you by directing the focus back to the early days of getting to know Him.

Over the years, there have been conflicting perspectives on who the Holy Spirit is, His attributes, and His role. Before reading the book *Good Morning, Holy Spirit* by Benny Hinn back in the nineties, the Holy Spirit was the third person of the Trinity with no real impact that I can remember in my day-to-day life. After reading his book, I would look forward to waking up in the morning and saying, "Good morning, Holy Spirit," and having a sense that I was beginning my day with Him.

Hearing how Benny Hinn embarked on this intimate relationship with the Holy Spirit shifted something in me as a new believer. I had entered the School of the Holy Spirit, daily learning to trust His leading, hear His promptings and being convicted of wrong thoughts and behaviours as I learned more about Jesus and living the Christian life.

I shared with you earlier that I prayed a Holy Spirit-led prayer in my bedroom, "Lord make me whole, make me who you created me to be." Can I tell you, I expected or hoped that I would have an immediate response, but I didn't. Over the coming years, I felt as though I had been stripped back to His original intent, not who or what I thought I was or wanted to be, or who I thought others wanted me to be. But He began to show me who I am in Him and then build me back up with Kingdom features.

In fact, I remember one day being in a meeting and I was laughing at a joke that someone had made when immediately in the recesses of my heart, I heard, "You don't even find that funny, why are you laughing?" I was startled, firstly, that this seemed like such a small thing, and then, secondly, what a strange thing to say. Yet, as always, the Holy Spirit was right on target. I had become so accustomed to trying to fit in that I had lost who I was and even what I thought was funny—because everyone else laughed, I laughed, too afraid to stand out.

From that day on, I would get prompt after prompt whenever I would revert to fitting in or hiding. Through that journey and the journey of writing poetry (something I had never done before coming to the Lord), I began to align with the Holy Spirit and God's will for my life. Please hear me when I say, I am not there yet; I am still on a journey to total obedience. There are still days I experience impostor syndrome. There are still days when I care more about what others are thinking than I do about what God is thinking or saying. That being said, in some areas of my life, I am unrecognisable from where I was, and so I am thankful for the journey and, most of all, for the leading and guiding of the Holy Spirit.

I am thankful because He has taught me and made me laugh (those stories are for another day or book). He has shown me what was to come and what will be coming. He has convicted me of sin, negative thinking and limiting beliefs. He has been present in the hard times and in the good times. He has taught me how to love, how to surrender, how to be more like Jesus.

He has taught me how to pray when I could not find the words; in seasons of pruning, the groans have been more articulate than any educated mind could string together.

The Holy Spirit, who I am writing about, is real, is needed and is the guide of all guides, if you will let Him into your life.

My prayer is that, as I have shared the unchanging, infallible, powerful Word of God with you in this Section, your foundation will be secure because no word from God will ever change (Luke 1:37). The Bible says, *"All Scripture is God-breathed and is useful for teaching, rebuking, correcting and training in righteousness."* (2 Timothy 3:16)

Now that you have a fuller understanding of who the Holy Spirit is from the Scriptures, you can more fully understand the analogy of the Sherpa we are going to explore in the next section.

You see, as I was studying about the Holy Spirit in 2018, the Lord said to me, "Go and begin to research Sherpas." As I did, I immediately began to see the correlation with the Holy Spirit, a revelation that has been transformational for me and many others.

So, go with me now to the next section to find out what the Holy Spirit revealed.

SECTION FOUR
The Holy Spirit...
Heaven's Sherpa

9

What or Who is a Sherpa?

As mentioned previously, this book is borne out of a teaching I first facilitated in 2018 for the International Wholeness Centre (IWC), which is when God gave me the analogy of the Holy Spirit as a Sherpa.

As I was preparing to teach on the Holy Spirit, I heard in the recesses of my heart, "I'm like a Heavenly Sherpa," and "I can take you to heights you cannot go alone." It arrested me for a moment because it is a concept I had never heard of before in all my Christian walk. So, I began musing on those words and, as usual, I said, "Show me where this is in your word." Anyone who has served with me for any period will know that while I embrace people's opinions as interesting and informative, I always want to see what Scripture has to say about whatever is being said or responded to. Why? Because my words can fade away, however, not one of God's words ever will (Matthew 5:18).

Immediately after I asked the Holy Spirit this question, I was reminded of Psalm 18:32-34 where David says, "*It is God who arms me with strength and keeps my way secure. He makes my feet like the feet of a deer; he causes me to stand on the heights.*

He trains my hands for battle; my arms can bend a bow of bronze."

The Scripture says it is God that makes my feet like the feet of a deer, it is Him who makes my way secure, and it is He that causes me to stand on heights. The Hebrew word for heights is *"bama"* and that means "high place, ridge, height, mountain, and battlefield". Just reading how my security is in God and that it is He who causes me to stand on heights gave me peace as I began to explore what and who Sherpas were. I was now ready to be introduced to the Holy Spirit as Heaven's Sherpa first.

Now that I have given you more insight into how the concept of the Holy Spirit as Heaven's Sherpa came about, join me to explore a bit about the role earthly Sherpas play in the lives of climbers, who depend on their expertise.

What or who is a Sherpa?

Before mountain climbing became a popular pastime in the Himalayas, the word Sherpa simply denoted a group of people who migrated to Nepal from Eastern Tibet. According to an article by CNN, the word originally meant "people from the East" and is pronounced *"shar-wa"* by the Sherpa themselves. This was before the two regions became separate countries.

According to the article, "Ethnic Sherpas established themselves in the mountains of Solukhumbu Valley in Nepal with the oldest community at Pangboche village. The valley is now a national park and the village a starting point for scaling Mount Everest – also known as Sagarmatha and Chomolungma – whose exact height has been recorded as 8,848 or 8,850 meters by separate geological agencies."

So, simply put, a Sherpa is a member of an ethnic group in the Himalayas. They are native to the mountainous regions of Nepal, Tibet, Bhutan, and parts of India and are known for their expertise in guiding climbers and trekkers through the challenging mountainous terrain of the region.

As well as their mountaineering skills and deep knowledge of the local mountains, Sherpas are renowned for their physical endurance. They have a long history of assisting mountaineering expeditions and have played a crucial role in the success of numerous climbs in the Himalayas, including those on Mount Everest, the world's highest peak.

Sherpas often serve as guides, carrying heavy loads, setting up camps, and assisting climbers in acclimatising to high altitudes. Their expertise and experience make them valuable members of mountaineering teams, providing physical, mental and emotional support, and ensuring the safety of climbers.

In recent years, the term "Sherpa" has also been used metaphorically to describe someone who guides or assists others in various domains, not necessarily related to mountaineering. For example, in business, a Sherpa may refer to a trusted advisor or mentor who helps navigate challenges and provides guidance along the way. Just as a Sherpa steers a climber safely towards triumph in the mountains, these metaphorical Sherpas help their clients, mentees and learners in attaining their aspirations, whether that is to acquire specific skills, knowledge or tangible outcomes. The term works well as a meaningful parallel because Sherpas possess a multitude of abilities similar to the support a person needs in order to get from one point to another with minimal setbacks.

Why do mountaineers need a Sherpa?

Mountaineers rely on Sherpas for a number of reasons, including but not limited to:

Local knowledge and experience

Sherpas have extensive knowledge of the local terrain, weather conditions, and the intricacies of the mountains. They have grown up in the region and are intimately familiar with the routes, hazards, and potential challenges. Their experience and understanding are invaluable for ensuring the safety and success of a climb.

High altitude expertise

Climbing at high altitudes presents unique challenges due to low oxygen levels and the risk of altitude sickness. Sherpas have adapted to these conditions and possess a remarkable ability to function at high altitudes. They understand how to acclimatise properly, recognise the symptoms of altitude sickness, and provide appropriate guidance to climbers.

Physical support

Sherpas are incredibly strong and capable of carrying heavy loads at high altitudes. They often act as porters, carrying essential equipment, supplies, and provisions for the climbers. This allows the mountaineers to focus on their own physical exertion without being burdened by excessive weight.

Setting up camps and fixing ropes

Sherpas are skilled in establishing base and higher camps, and fixing ropes along the climbing routes. They assist in the logistics of establishing secure and functional campsites, ensuring that climbers have suitable places to rest and recover during their ascent. They may also fix ropes on challenging sections, such as steep or icy slopes, making it easier and safer for the climbers to progress.

Safety and emergency assistance

Sherpas play a crucial role in ensuring the safety of climbers. They are trained in first aid and rescue techniques, and their presence increases the chances of a timely response in case of accidents or emergencies. They are experienced in identifying potential risks and can make decisions to mitigate dangers or turn back if conditions become too hazardous.

Overall, Sherpas' combination of local knowledge, mountaineering expertise, physical strength, and dedication to their craft makes them indispensable for mountaineering expeditions in the Himalayas. They provide essential support, guidance, and safety measures that greatly increase the chances of a successful and safe climb.

Clearly, there are several good reasons why God sent the Holy Spirit to help us on our walk and to ensure we reach the summit of our spiritual journey safely, just as a Sherpa guides and supports climbers to reach the highest peaks.

When I reflect on the similarities of the Holy Spirit and the role of a Sherpa, I am amazed, because it gives us such a clear example of what we have access to and so often fail to tap into. The analogy demonstrates how much we need the Holy Spirt in every area of our lives; just like a mountaineer needs a Sherpa to guide and lead, so do we need Heaven's Sherpa.

10

Why We Need the Holy Spirit... Heaven's Sherpa

A person could not survive a potentially dangerous mountainous terrain without having a Sherpa to guide them. Similarly, many people have suffered casualties because they failed to draw on the guidance of the Holy Spirit. We will touch on a few of these as we continue to explore this topic.

I believe there are some high places God wants to take you to, some unventured realms in worship, elevated levels in government and politics, pinnacles in education, spiritual heights in religion, deep breakthroughs in family, peaks in business, and summits in the realms of arts and entertainment— if you will only wait on Heaven's Sherpa.

Today and in the coming days, to impact this earth for the Kingdom, we need Holy Spirit-led mountain climbers, people who will answer God's call with an unreserved "Yes, here I am, send me," without thought for safety or ability because their trust is in the One who has gone before them. I believe the Holy Spirit is ready (and has always been ready) to equip, teach and guide an army of believers who will fully rely on His leading into the fresh supernatural terrain that is necessary to win the souls of many who currently see no need for God. This may mean doing unusual things, it may mean that there are fewer of you on the trek, but the outcome will be Kingdom expansion.

As I wrote those words, I was reminded of a time when I was prompted to ask someone to perform an unusual task, even though I didn't understand why. We were in a JPIM prayer meeting and towards the end of the meeting I sensed that we should form a human wall. I then asked one of the volunteers there to run around the room. I had no idea at the time what was going to happen next, only that I was inspired to instruct her to run. She ran and then after a short while she began to say, "I'm tired." Yet, I knew she could not give up, she had to just keep running. She continued, gasping and now starting to run out of steam when the Holy Spirit prompted me to tell her to break through the human wall. I also told everyone not to make it easy for her. She tried to push her way forward and was truly weary but, eventually, broke through to the cheers of all present.

Let me tell you, even after we concluded our time together, I had no idea why we did that or why she was the focus. Within weeks, this lady was diagnosed with an aggressive form of breast cancer and entered a season of chemotherapy. I now understood why she was singled out and had to press through even when she was tired: she was going to have to fight this cancer, and even when she felt she was running out of steam, persevere towards her breakthrough. Praise be to God, she fought and triumphed: that was about ten years ago as of today and she is still cancer-free.

Why am I sharing this? Because to ascend to high places with the Holy Spirit, Heaven's Sherpa, you must trust His leading, even when it makes little sense, even when you have to stand alone for a while, even when you feel weary or discouraged. Trusting our guide is non-negotiable for a smooth journey because you cannot go alone, you need someone who knows the terrain, someone who understands the risks, who knows what you carry now and what you have the potential to carry. You need someone who knows what is ahead and more. You need the Holy Spirit, Heaven's Sherpa.

Guidance and local knowledge (and knowledge of the terrain)

Another thing I found interesting about Sherpas is their role as guides at extreme altitudes of peaks and passes. Do you see that? Are you getting this? Sherpas function at extreme altitudes in the natural; the Holy Spirit operates at extreme altitudes in the Heavenly realm—and yet He resides in you! That's powerful! The Holy Spirit possesses an intimate knowledge of Heaven's corridors, streets and pathways. He knows the terrain, passes and rocky roads implicitly. This innate knowledge of Heaven's rugged and impassable terrains and exploits makes the Holy Spirit an expert guide.

In addition to a Sherpa's local knowledge is their sensitivity to predict what the weather is likely to be like. They know when a storm is gathering. They know when an avalanche is imminent because they have become accustomed to the atmospheric signs. Just as earthly Sherpas know the terrain of the mountains, the Holy Spirit knows the terrain of spiritual realms. He will warn you when He sees a spiritual storm coming your way. He knows when the enemy is setting up an avalanche for you or attempting to lead you along perilous paths where your foot will fall. He knows, and that is why we need His guidance as Heaven's Sherpa.

Some of us have been going through personal avalanches, and geysers have dropped on us in life. Often, we have found ourselves in these situations because we didn't access the help of our Heavenly Sherpa to guide us, to lead us, to say, "This is the way to go," or "No, no, no, don't stop there, keep moving." Many of us have missed out on His precise strategic instructions that would have whispered, "This isn't the time to give in" or encouraged, "This is the time to press through." The Holy Spirit foresaw these trials and always knows what it will take to help us to persevere ahead.

After the pandemic in 2020, many believers didn't return to church, deciding to wander away or take a different path. Likewise, many pastors left their calling and have not looked back. Just as those who have remained on their assignment need Heaven's Sherpa to continue to stand strong, those individuals who have left or stopped participating in the Kingdom's work need Him to help them navigate through these unprecedented times. The Holy Spirit knew the pandemic was coming, and He knew what it would take to preserve those who have been climbing. Praise be to God that we are on this side of it, but we know we can trust Him when the next avalanche comes—and come it will.

To those who are on the side-lines, those who have found comfort sitting behind their screens, we are glad you stayed but please know that the mission still requires your participation. It isn't too late to re-engage, to pick up your weapons, don your armour and begin climbing again. God still has need of you. You have rested long enough; you have sat observing from the side-lines enough. It is time to step back in the expedition because there is a place waiting just for you. Selah…

Here is the encouraging truth for those who are willing to answer the call to resume the climb: you will not have to do it alone. Heaven's Sherpa will tell God's spiritual mountaineers where to stop, where to rest, when to continue and where to turn. Some of us have not rested long enough and are wondering why we are burning out. We are wondering why we feel drained and are living in regret or—if we really keep it real—with resentment. We are asking questions like, "Why haven't I been promoted?", "Why am I still in debt?", "When will I get married?", "Why aren't I healed yet?", and the list goes on. Too many of God's children are walking around smiling on the outside yet dying on the inside.

It is time to access Heaven's Sherpa for your situation and allow Him to take you to the places He has promised. Beyond our desires, He also wants to show us how to cure some stubborn situations in our churches, communities and nations. He wants to show us how to get delivered in areas of our lives plagued with dis-ease, discomfort and dissatisfaction. He wants to show us, but we must first get in line with the Spirit of the Living God. It is time to surrender to the lead of Heaven's Sherpa.

I know some people might be reading this and saying, "I am in line. I've done everything I know to do, yet still I'm not experiencing the supernatural. I'm not experiencing peace in my family, my phone hasn't rung for ministry engagements, and I'm living in a place I have long outgrown. Still, I am serving and serving and serving and not making headway. Still…" You finish the sentence.

If the truth be told, there are times when God wants to give us time to rest but, instead, we busy ourselves. There are also times He offers us direction but we are too busy doing nonessentials, claiming lack of time or taking time off.

If we follow the leading of the Holy Spirit, Heaven's Sherpa, we will rest at the right junctures, we will work at the right times, we will go when we need to go or wait when we need to wait, all with a sense of peace. Why? Because He's the guide. He will never guide us off course or out of season. He knows the local area, the terrain and the heights of Heaven. He knows when a flood or storm is coming and how that storm will affect us. We need Him.

Before I carry on, I want to pause to repent. Please join me if you feel prompted to do so.

Father, forgive me. I repent of all the times I have gone ahead of Your Spirit, all the times I have made my own decisions and left you out of the equation. Forgive me for the times I have felt resentful or dissatisfied because an outcome wasn't what I had hoped and, in some cases, prayed for. Forgive me, I'm sorry. I'm sorry for making other voices, including my own, louder than Yours. Forgive me. I repent and ask you to lead me, to be Heaven's Sherpa in my life, moment by moment, hour by hour, day by day. I need You. I pray in Jesus' name. Amen.

I hope you prayed this simple prayer of repentance with me so that we can begin afresh and travel to the heights God has for us.

The journey – route planner

On any expedition, it is the Sherpa who plans the route for the mountaineers. While the mountaineers are sleeping or resting the Sherpa is awake, determining the best route to take.

The Bible depicts a similar scenario in Psalms 121 (NKJV), where it describes how our God is ever awake and watching out for His children:

> I will lift up my eyes to the hills—
> From whence comes my help?
> My help comes from the Lord,
> Who made heaven and earth.
>
> He will not allow your foot to be moved;
> He who keeps you will not slumber.
> Behold, He who keeps Israel
> Shall neither slumber nor sleep.
>
> The Lord is your keeper;
> The Lord is your shade at your right hand.
> The sun shall not strike you by day,
> Nor the moon by night.
> The Lord shall preserve you from all evil;
> He shall preserve your soul.
> The Lord shall preserve your going out and your coming in
> From this time forth, and even forevermore.

Our God neither sleeps nor slumbers; He protects us from evil, keeps us as we come and go, and will not allow our steps to slip. He will secure the path before us and ensure that we are not taken out before our time. What an amazing description of our help from Heaven here on Earth.

Can you imagine the conversations between the Sherpas:

"Let's take the north track because it looks like the storms coming in from the east and we can avoid it if we go there."

"Tommy doesn't look like he can make that route, let's circle back to the west path and navigate our way up through there."

Both Earth's Sherpas and Heaven's Sherpa share a common trait: their extensive knowledge of the journey ahead, because of having made the trek many times. They know the pitfalls and potential hazards and are adept at manoeuvring around them to ensure a safe ascent. The difference between them lies in the fact that Heaven's Sherpa also knows exactly what you can handle, how far you can go and how much you can carry. He knows you at your deepest level—your destiny, calling and gifts. As a result, He can chart a journey that perfectly matches your life. That's why we need the Holy Spirit; not only is He familiar with who we are, where we are and where we are going, but he also knows about the potholes and the distractions and possesses the tools and equipment necessary for your specific climb.

The Sherpas get the equipment ready for everyone to move to the next dimension. This means that the minute the mountaineers awaken from their rest, the Sherpas can say, "Come, this is the way to go." If we are not careful and fail to listen keenly to the Heavenly Sherpa, we might respond, "But I thought we were going to go that way." We start to override the expert—the Holy Spirit. We are guilty of doing this more than we care to admit, overriding His unction when He said, "Sell now", "Buy now", "Pick that up", "Don't pick it up." We dismiss His prompting and then we sit down and have a pity party saying, "I've been praying for the last twenty years for this thing, and it's just not working." Meanwhile, the Holy Spirit is saying, "I want to show you the terrain but you're not letting me." We become so used to doing things our way. We become "professional Christians", or worse, can be so full of pride and not even realise it. We have the God of the universe living in us, yet we can make decisions devoid of His leading.

I recall one day while I was in America many years ago. I was sitting in a Sunday service and as the preacher was preaching, I heard the words in my spirit, "We are acting like the shepherd and treating God like the sheep." I was taken aback because the preacher wasn't preaching about the shepherd or sheep so when that thought came to me, it got my attention. It was, and dare I say, is, so true. We make plans and then ask God to sanction them, rather than asking Him where He wants to lead us and following His direction.

Are you the shepherd or is the Lord your Shepherd?

Although we might all want to answer that the Lord is indeed our Shepherd, our behaviour often demonstrates a different picture. Some of us cannot even take directions without getting frustrated with the person giving them, thinking we know the way or could do it quicker or better. Lord, forgive us for the sin of pride!

Around eleven or twelve years ago, having gone to lunch with two of my pastors at the time, I was driving us back to the office. We had gone to a restaurant in an area that was familiar to me, but not a place I went to often. As we were driving, one of them said, "Turn here," to which I responded, "It's okay, I know where I'm going," only to end up on a dead-end road, because the road layout had changed. It made me think, how often do we tell God, "Not now," or "It's okay, I've got this," only to end up in a dead-end relationship, job or situation?

I do not believe God is looking for titles or positions, but for people who will humble themselves before their God and walk uprightly. He is looking for people who will submit to the leading of the Heavenly Sherpa and, as we do, He will unveil exactly how to address issues in our lives, families, churches, communities and nations. Some of us have needed deliverance and healing for as long as we can remember, and God wants to heal us. Yet when He tells us to do something that isn't comfortable to our flesh, like exercise or change our eating habits, we hesitate or complain or let pride enter.

God is looking for people who will submit to the One who knows the way, knows the terrain and the path. To follow someone else's lead takes humility. Whether it is for directions on the road, how to use a computer package or on a greater more life-changing level, it takes a heart of submission to a God who is all-knowing and all-seeing to be willing to submit.

The Holy Spirit knows the plans God the Father has for you. He knows that they are good, and not of evil, plans that will prosper you and give you a hope and a future (see Jeremiah 29:11). Whilst this Scripture relates to the nation of Israel as opposed to an individual, over the years, Christians have taken comfort in the knowledge that God knows the plans He has for us too; if He cares about numbering the hairs on our head (Luke 12:7), He certainly cares about the plans He has for us.

Safety and emergency assistance

Do you know what I love? Research shows that Sherpas take care of the distribution of the baggage. Sherpas are small in physical stature, yet they can carry up to twenty-five kilos worth of equipment and luggage. These people can carry a heavy weight, and they will also assess who can carry what safely, before distributing luggage to each person. Did you catch that? The Sherpas assess who can carry what and do so based on their experience. It is not because someone is bigger than someone else or more experienced; they have inbuilt discernment and distribute as they will. They look at Suzy and say, "She can carry three bags." Then they look at Tommy and start praying in tongues, saying, "This one can't carry much, give him two little bags." To the next they give one bag and so on, until all the equipment necessary for the climb is fairly distributed. Our Heavenly Sherpa, the Holy Spirit, knows what you can carry safely.

Likewise, the Bible says the Holy Spirit distributes gifts to each of us as He wills (1 Corinthians 12:11). The Holy Spirit knows the spiritual load you can safely carry. He equips you accordingly for each situation so you can resist the temptation to become diverted by the world or begin thinking that the anointing you have been given is for you, instead of those He called you to serve. He does not give us more than we can bear, and if it feels so, maybe it is time to look to Heaven's Sherpa.

When we do not understand or appreciate this, we can get into competition with who has how many bags (gifts, followers, congregants, etc.). Sometimes we are looking at others saying, "How come they've got all of that, and all I've got is this?" You have no idea what is in the "this"—in other words, what is inside their bag. We have overlooked the fact that it is the Holy Spirit, Heaven's Sherpa, who determines who can carry what. Can I keep it real for a moment? I am telling you, some of us should be giving God praise like never before because He didn't give you what you thought you wanted.

During my early years as a Christian, I would attend crowded meetings and conferences where I sat near the back, uncomfortable because the places were so packed. I would listen to the speakers at these events introducing their husbands, wives and other ministers who seemed to be sitting unencumbered at the front. I would think to myself, how I would love one of those front seats. Fast forward ten years after uttering those words, and I found that those seats can be costly—emotionally, spiritually, mentally and more. No one mentioned the cost of ministry.

To this day, I move away from those front seats unless called or assigned, because I know what it carries and costs to sit there. I know what I am saying when I state that some of us should be praising God that we are not carrying the "this" or "that" we are looking at from over here (whatever you are still wanting for). He knows the timing.

If we are not careful, we will look and say, "Oh, that one's little (in length of service, stature, education, Bible knowledge, ability), he can't carry much." But the Holy Spirit knows what He has deposited in that seemingly small frame; He knows what is in him. Sometimes we think it is the big (status, title, position, role, education, etc.) ones who should carry the most, but while we humans look at outward appearances, God looks at the heart (1 Samuel 16:7).

Once, I read a book by Rick Joyner called *The Final Quest*. He spoke about an experience he had of God taking Him to Heaven. In that heavenly vision, he saw some of the biggest TV evangelists who he expected to have the grandest mansions, but they didn't. There were some seemingly insignificant and unremarkable people there, people who never stood out on Earth. He saw a widow and different people occupying significant positions and enquired about them, only to find out that they were everyday people who just obeyed God. They stayed in their lanes; they didn't try to become preachers if that wasn't their calling; they didn't try to become businessmen or women, if that wasn't on God's agenda. They just stayed in their lane and prayed when God led them to pray. Now here they were in Heaven experiencing the glory because they listened to Heaven's Sherpa. They listened to what He said to do and didn't try to become anything other than who God called them to be. Significantly, they didn't try to carry anything more than what God requested of them.

Sherpas help support climbers when they have accidents. They are trained in first aid and will administer it correctly to ensure the expedition continues. Think about that—if earthly Sherpas are trained to administer first aid, how much more is our Heavenly Sherpa, the Holy Spirit, who knows the healing we need, who knows the antidote for every virus, infection, outbreak or bruise you have ever experienced or ever will.

According to CBS News, every year, five people die while out mountaineering. Having a Sherpa does not guarantee that you will survive the climb. When I read this, I realised that no matter how much Sherpas do for us here on Earth, following them and sticking with them does not guarantee success. However, we have a Heavenly Sherpa that sticks closer than a brother, who is living on the inside of you waiting for you to obey. Wow! I hope and pray you are recognising what power you have within, what access to God you have on the inside of you. I pray that you are resetting any preconceived ideas and fears about who your Heavenly Sherpa is. I hope that you are reassessing His role in your life and saying, "Holy Spirit, Heaven's Sherpa, lead me."

A couple of lyrics from "Oceans", a song by Hillsong, has come to me several times as I have been writing. The lyrics have become a prayer that I pray we will all embrace as we ask the Holy Spirit to lead us where we can trust Him without boundaries. If you know that song, it asks the Holy Spirit to lead us where trust has no limitations. It talks of walking on the water, just like Peter did before he took his eyes off Jesus. It prays for a walk that is deeper than our "feet could ever wander", one that will cause our faith to become stronger. And all of this because we allow Heaven's Sherpa to lead us. I know I desire a life like this, do you?

High altitude expertise

Climbing at high altitudes presents unique challenges due to low oxygen levels and the risk of altitude sickness. Sherpas can manage this well because they have developed a genetic adaptation to living in high altitudes. Specific research published in the *National Library of Medicine* in 1976 found that due to Sherpas' prolonged exposure to high altitudes when compared to acclimatised Caucasians, they have a higher affinity of blood to oxygen. Their system has adapted to enable them to survive at higher altitudes. *My, my, my, there is something about their blood.*

When I read this, I immediately thought about the blood of Jesus that was sacrificially shed for us—it gives us access to a multitude of benefits, including an eternal home in Heaven. Just as the blood of Sherpas empowers them to navigate the heights and altitudes that others cannot, the blood of Jesus grants us access to Heaven's Sherpa, the Holy Spirit. It was Jesus who said,

"I will ask the Father, and He will give you another Helper (Comforter, Advocate, Intercessor—Counsellor, Strengthener,

Standby), to be with you forever—the Spirit of Truth, whom the world cannot receive [and take to its heart] because it does not see Him or know Him, but you know Him because He (the Holy Spirit) remains with you continually and will be in you." {John 14:16, AMP)

How powerful! The Spirit of Christ, also known as the Spirit of Truth and the Holy Spirit, is with us.

Let me tell you, when you are endowed with the Holy Spirit, you will be able to operate at high altitudes. People will wonder how you can manage what you do: it is because you are Holy-Ghost-genetically-modified, where the Holy Spirit has taken an active role in shifting and turning you, shaping your character and guiding your actions. I know I want to operate there. I want to operate at Heavenly altitudes, how about you?

I believe the Holy Spirit wants to come alive and afresh in your life. I believe He wants to re-ignite those prophetic dreams and promises you have received. He wants to become a living and active force in your life to the extent that when you walk, even your shadow has an impact. With Him in control, when you talk, you will become a solutionist to nations and generations. Why? Because you learned to operate at Heaven's altitude.

Allow me to illustrate. A couple of years ago, I was at a revival meeting that Dr Brad and Pastor Wyona were hosting, when the fire of God hit me. It is a feeling that is difficult to describe but felt like a bolt hit me. My chest felt like it was bursting with joy and as much as I wanted to be dignified, I could not help but laugh, almost uncontrollably. Then, the preacher put the mic to my mouth and asked me to explain what was happening to me, but I could hardly speak. I managed to utter, "I'm combusting, my heart's combusting, my heart's combusting." I have pictures to prove it; they are not pretty but very, very real.

I was awake in bed around 2:00 am the following morning when the Holy Spirit said, "You don't use that word 'combust', what does it mean?" I was like, "I don't even know what it means." I then tried to articulate it but could not. The word just came out of my spirit when the preacher asked me what was happening to me. I looked it up and found that the word means, "to destroy or to be consumed by fire". I then heard the words, "Daughter, everything that is not of you now has been destroyed by fire, now you're consumed by My holy fire."

Wow! Words you didn't even know will come out of your mouth, simply because you have allowed the Holy Spirit to have full reign in your life. You will know how to do things you didn't know you could do, simply because the Holy Spirit has downloaded the spiritual manual to your spirit.

CAUTION: Giving God full reign of your life does not mean acting out of control and being unaware of what you are doing. Remember the teaching in 1 Corinthians 14:32, which says, "The spirits of prophets are subject to the control of prophets." So, as He leads, there will be a witness to let you know it is of Him. We have all seen the unusual and seemingly ridiculous in the body of Christ over the years, so I am always careful to "test the spirits" lest I rebuke what God has sanctioned or run away with what He hasn't (1 John 4:1). So, for the one who feels afraid of surrendering, be encouraged; whatever is of Him will remain, whatever is of Him will be supported by His Word, the holy Scriptures. Whatever is of Him should be and can be tested by wise counsel.

THE HOLY SPIRIT... HEAVEN'S SHERPA

I believe that God wants to heal some of you afresh as you enter a renewed relationship with the Holy Spirit. You have operated on empty for far too long. You have operated on "my way" and "their way" instead of "His way". Some of you believe, because of what you have been taught, that "it's just the way I've always done it" or "it's just the way it's always been". I want to challenge you, sometimes what we have always done, is what we have always done. But can I say, for some of you, it no longer works. What you have always done has found you in a place where you are more tired. You are wearier, more critical, more frustrated. Some of you are just going through the motions of life because you have outgrown that space. The Bible says that you can be filled with the Holy Spirit and that we all ought to be filled with Him. But we must expect Him, and we must know Him. That is the number one thing.

Setting up camps and fixing ropes

Sherpas are skilled in establishing and assisting with the logistics of securing functional campsites. They fix ropes along the climbing routes and on challenging sections, such as steep or icy slopes, making it easier and safer for the climbers to progress.

As I read about this attribute of a Sherpa, how they are skilled at establishing campsites and assisting in the logistics of secure and functional sites both at base and higher levels, I thought about how much we need the Holy Spirit, Heaven's Sherpa, in our churches and ministries.

He is needed in the place (campsites) where we tabernacle each Sunday and for midweek services and events. We need His guidance on how we ought to steward His church, and how we should structure it so that it is secure for those He has planted there to grow and progress. We need secure and functional ministries that are fully trusting in His leading, so that when He says to build outwards, we build outwards; if He says build online, we build online. If He instructs us to build a place where people can go deep, begin digging deeper because Heaven's Sherpa is aware of what we carry and who and where He wants us to impact and grow.

Just think how critical it is when Sherpas fix those ropes along the climbing route, especially those challenging sections where it is steep or icy. All along our way, the Holy Spirit is handing us ropes to help us with the journey, yet because those ropes can sometimes look like hard work, or have come through those we didn't expect, we ignore them, only to take a fall.

I want to encourage you to begin looking for the ropes the Holy Spirit is sending you. They may be ropes of Bible study so you can know Him, the Father and the Son more deeply and intimately. It may be a rope of leadership, where God has placed you in a campsite where you can grow. Pray and ask the Holy Spirit, "Show me the ropes I need and how to set up camp (ministry) safely, securely and functionally so that I, and those I serve, can climb to higher heights and deeper depths in You."

The article I read on Sherpas said that there are base campsites and higher campsites, each one playing its own important role during different stages of the climb. Some of you have spent too long too low, and God is sending you a rope of a position of service in your campsite. Please hear me and hear me well: ministry is about service, whatever your office, whatever your role or title. It is service, and sometimes we just have to grab a rope and pull in whatever direction the Holy Spirit is leading.

Heaven's Sherpa may be sending you a rope of counsel, where you have been challenged with some emotional and mental traumas for too long. Though you have prayed, the root of the trauma hasn't been addressed. Take that rope; if He's handing you an opportunity to be well, take it; if it is a rope to pull you up higher, respond to it. As I just wrote that, I saw an image of a drowning person being thrown a rope to grab hold of, so they can be saved. Some are drowning in sin, disappointment and regret—but reach out to the rope of hope today, in Jesus' name.

The rope the Holy Spirit is securing for you may be one of prayer and fasting, because that is what will ensure your successful climb to your next season. Whatever kind of rope you need, Heaven's Sherpa is well-equipped to supply because He sees the steeps, He sees the slopes, and He sees the lows. He knows that you will avoid these when you receive His divine direction.

Prayer

One of the key traditions of Sherpas is to pray before any expedition. Most Sherpas practice a form of Tibetan Buddhism, which has a strong influence on their daily lives. They follow Buddhist teachings and rituals, including chanting mantras, spinning prayer wheels, and making offerings to their deities. Before each expedition, they religiously pray a prayer called the *puja* and they will not start climbing until they have done this.

Some of us start climbing only to realise when we are halfway up and dangling that we have not prayed. Yet earthly Sherpas know that before they begin to climb, they have not only got to pray but also give up their tithes and offerings. Wow! Before embarking on these potentially treacherous journeys, they perform rituals and prayers seeking protection and safe passage from the mountain deities.

Do you know, some of us are in a place right now of our own doing. Can I keep it real? The devil didn't put you where you are—very often it is us who put ourselves in untenable positions. We have moved without prayer; we have set up stuff that God never asked us to set up, all because we failed to pray. We have withheld giving without prayer and then we can be heard crying out, "Lord! Why hath thou forsaken me!" When God never led you to that particular mountain.

Do not stop praying, and when you do not know what to pray, remember Heaven's Sherpa, the Holy Spirit, will intercede on your behalf (Romans 8:26).

I find it so sad that we have access to everything we have need of through prayer and yet on too many occasions, we resort to prayer as a final act. What do I mean? When we are going through a challenging time and someone asks, "What are you going to do," and we respond with platitudes like, "I can't do anything else but pray" or "This or that didn't come through so I'm just going to have to pray," like prayer is the last resort instead of our first port of call. The Sherpa does not attempt an expedition without praying to their god for protection, guidance and security. Yet, we who know the true and living God too often put prayer below our works.

Please forgive my candidness as I write—I just want us to wake up. I want us to see what power, what opportunity, what privilege, what a gift we have in Heaven's Sherpa, the Holy Spirit, so we can climb to the heights we know we are born to reach.

THE HOLY SPIRIT... HEAVEN'S SHERPA

I pray with everything in me that you catch this revelation. You have a Helper, God Himself, dwelling on the inside of you, filling you, leading you, directing you—if you will just yield to His Lordship in your life.

Do you know one of my prayers for this book as I write? It is that a sound would begin to be heard throughout the earth, like the sound made in the days of Ezekiel when the dead dried bones of an army began to reassemble. The account in Ezekiel 37 tells us that when Heaven's Sherpa led the prophet Ezekiel to the valley, he heeded the Word of the Lord and began to prophesy life into those dried-up bones. The Bible records Ezekiel as saying, *"So I prophesied as I was commanded; and as I prophesied, there was a [thundering] noise, and behold, a rattling; and the bones came together, bone to its bone."*

Oh, can you hear the tremendous sound of born-again, spirit-filled believers around the globe, beginning to move as they are led, beginning to climb the peaks of the 7 Mountains of Influence[1] in the world? Oh, I can!

According to an article on the BBC's website, British mountaineer Kenton Cool, who has climbed Everest 11 times, explains: "The Sherpas are so important. For one, they're the local people, so they know the culture, they know the area, they know the people. But when it actually comes to climbing the mountain, they have this phenomenal energy and power on the mountain. They really are the backbone of any expedition."

---

1   The 7 Mountains of Influence refer to seven key societal sectors or domains that have a significant impact on shaping culture and society. These are: Religion, Family, Education, Government, Media, Arts & Entertainment, and Business. They are often discussed in the context of leadership, influence, and cultural transformation.

The Holy Spirit is the backbone of your expeditions. He is indeed the One with phenomenal energy and power to position you to climb in this season, and any to come.

The HOLY SPIRIT wants to lead you, guide you, show you the route planned for you, and help you avoid dangerous terrains in the spirit... If we will trust the leading of Heaven's Sherpa, some of those obstacles and heartaches we have experienced along the way, that could have been avoided or had a lesser impact, will not become part of our future. Just like earthly Sherpas know where the danger lies and plan the safest routes for ascent, so shall our Heavenly Sherpa.

If we are to be revived, restored, reawakened, refreshed and breathed into afresh... we need the Holy Spirit! We need Heaven's Sherpa!

SECTION FIVE
Cultivating Your Relationship with the Holy Spirit

11

Cultivating Your Relationship - Biblical Examples

So far, we have looked at some of my early encounters with the Holy Spirit and how one encounter can change everything. We have taken time to study who the Holy Spirit is, establishing a Biblical foundation upon which to build our relationship. And we have looked at the Holy Spirit as Heaven's Sherpa.

In this last section, our focus shifts to cultivating our relationship with the Holy Spirit so that as we go through our Christian life, we can be assured of His presence, His function, His attributes and more.

The word "cultivate" is a verb that means to foster or nurture the growth and development of something, whether it be physical, intellectual, emotional, or spiritual. It is often used to describe the deliberate and careful effort put into the improvement of a skill, quality, relationship, or any other aspect of life.

When you cultivate something, you work on it over time, giving it the attention, care, and resources it needs to flourish and reach its full potential. The process of cultivation involves dedication, patience, and perseverance.

Let us begin with a few Biblical examples of people who cultivated a strong relationship with Heaven's Sherpa. Their stories will help us to learn some fundamental keys to enhancing our own relationship.

Philip

Acts 8:26-40 tells the story of Philip, one of the early followers of Jesus, who is led by the Holy Spirit to encounter an Ethiopian eunuch returning from worship in Jerusalem. The eunuch is reading from the Book of Isaiah, and Philip, prompted by the Holy Spirit, approaches him and explains the passage, using it as an opportunity to share the Gospel of Jesus Christ. The eunuch is receptive to the message and desires to be baptised, which Philip performs. After the baptism, Philip is taken away by the Holy Spirit, and the eunuch continues his journey with joy, having received the message of salvation.

For me, this encounter beautifully describes one of the most important ways we can cultivate our relationship with the Holy Spirit, and that is through obedience. I shared in my early encounters with the Holy Spirit how, at times, even though my flesh wrestled with the leading of the Holy Spirit, when I obeyed, it deepened my relationship as I learned to trust Him more and more. I see this in Philip's story. As soon as the Holy Spirit told Philip to approach the eunuch's chariot and to stay near it, he moved—no hesitation, no double guessing, just pure obedience. The Bible says that Philip ran to the chariot, which gave me the sense that he didn't want to miss his assignment; he wanted to move as the Holy Spirit led him. No doubt, Philip would have been cultivating this relationship beforehand, and so the Holy Spirit knew he could be trusted with this assignment.

Philip shows us how obedience is key to cultivating a relationship with the Holy Spirit, a lesson we can all learn. However, it isn't the only lesson: Philip's story highlights another key to cultivating a relationship with the Holy Spirit, which is to be ready to move as He leads.

In verses 39-40 of Acts 8, we see the Holy Spirit suddenly take Philip away, and the eunuch never sees him again. Philip was next seen in Azotus, travelling about preaching and teaching the Gospel in all the towns until he reached Caesarea. Philip didn't build a tabernacle by the water where he baptised the eunuch or build altars there praising God for the eunuch's life—not that that is a bad idea. The point is that Philip was immediately ready to move. He didn't wait to catch his breath, he completed his assignment, and he was off. As the Holy Spirit led, he moved.

Whilst close to my earlier lesson about obedience, I see something slightly different in the promptness in which Philip obeyed and was ready to be led. He made no excuses. We see how easily people make excuses for doing what God is calling them to do. For example, in the parable of the great banquet in Luke 14:15-23, the host of the banquet sends his servants to invite people to the feast, and one by one they make excuses: "I have just bought a field." "I have just bought five oxen, I'm on my way to try them out." "I've just got married, so I can't come." Excuses, excuses, excuses.

I wonder how many times the Holy Spirit has called you to do something with the potential to enlarge the Kingdom of God, even if it was just to help one person, and you have reeled off excuses. Had Philip not immediately gone, I wonder if he would have arrived at the right portion of Scripture that the eunuch was reading in Isaiah? Would he have been baptised by the water at just that point? We could carry on with the "what if's" but there is no need because not only was Philip obedient, but he also moved promptly, without excuse.

If you are to grow in your relationship with the Holy Spirit, you must move when He leads, not in your own time, but in His.

I will give you an example. In my early years as a Christian when I was learning to cultivate my relationship with the Holy Spirit (and, if the truth be told, I am still on that journey daily as He reveals Himself in different ways at different times), I went through a season when I would feel a prompting to wake up every morning at around 5:00 am. I shared this with a fellow Christian and they suggested it could be God prompting me to get up to pray. Excited that the Holy Spirit was speaking to me, I obliged for the first couple of days until the warmth and the comfort of my bed started to give me an excuse. I would say, "I'll get up in a minute." I even remember saying to the Lord, "Can we talk between nine to five, during office hours—why so early?" I'm sure you know what I am talking about. How many times have *you* bargained with God? Maybe it wasn't about rising early, perhaps it was about stepping into the position He is calling you to, supporting the ministry He has assigned you to, sharing your gift in your community, or something else.

So, our lesson from Philip is that he demonstrated the keys to cultivating an intimate relationship with the Holy Spirit by moving promptly when he was led—because partial obedience is disobedience.

Jesus

Jesus, being fully divine (God) and fully human (man), had a unique relationship with the Holy Spirit. Though they are co-equal and co-eternal, Jesus fully surrendered Himself to the will of the Father and allowed the Holy Spirit to empower Him for

His mission. John 14:16-17 says, *"And I will ask the Father, and he will give you another advocate to help you and be with you forever—the Spirit of truth."*

This text speaks to me of surrender and humility. To truly cultivate a relationship with the Holy Spirit, we must be humble and surrender to His leading. It cannot be a case of "my will and a bit of His will". An intimate relationship with Heaven's Sherpa calls for a humble heart that seeks the Father's will entirely. Remember, He knows the journey, He knows the steep hills, and He knows when those storms are coming.

Jesus knew His mission on Earth was coming to an end for now and He was humble enough to hand over to another advocate that would help us and be with us forever, the Holy Spirit, the Spirit of truth.

In Luke 4:1-2, we see the Holy Spirit leading Jesus into the wilderness to be tempted by the devil for forty days and forty nights. This wasn't a comfortable place. I once heard my nephew preach a powerful message about Jesus being led to a place of discomfort. He said some of us without a doubt would question whether the Holy Spirit had spoken to us in the first place. There is something about us that wants comfort, ease and to flee from pain, yet if the truth be told, we only need to look at our Saviour's life and journey to the cross to realise that life as a Christian does not always lead to ease. However, it always leads to eternal life and multiple blessings (Psalm 103, John 10:10, 14:2).

Jesus' example serves as an inspiration and model for us to cultivate our own relationships with the Holy Spirit through prayer, dependence, obedience, and surrender to God's will.

Paul

The Apostle Paul, previously known as Saul of Tarsus, was a devout Jewish Pharisee who vehemently opposed the followers of Jesus and actively persecuted Christians. However, during his journey to Damascus to arrest the followers of Christ, he experienced a dramatic conversion. After this encounter, Paul was temporarily blinded and led into the city of Damascus by his companions. In Damascus, he met a Christian named Ananias, who had been instructed by the Lord in a vision to lay hands on Paul's eyes so he would receive his sight and, right then, something like scales fell from his eyes. The Bible says he not only received his sight but was also baptised and filled with the Holy Spirit (Acts 9:17-18).

From that moment on, Paul became a devoted follower of Christ and dedicated his life to spreading the Gospel throughout various regions of the world. Apostle Paul was also divinely inspired and led by the Holy Spirit to teach, preach and write the majority of the New Testament. This brings me to another key to cultivating a relationship with the Holy Spirit, observed through Paul's journey.

To cultivate a relationship with the Holy Spirit, you must be filled by Him. After Ananias laid hands on him, the Bible says Paul was filled with the Holy Spirit. As mentioned earlier, the minute we become believers, the Holy Spirit comes to live within us. Yet the Bible also talks about being filled by the Holy Spirit, so to develop a deep relationship with the Holy Spirit, you must both receive and be filled by Him (Acts 4:31, Ephesians 5:18).

Your relationship with the Holy Spirit will result in your service to make Jesus famous. The role of the Holy Spirit, as we have already established in why He came, is to speak of Jesus and remind us of what Jesus has said. This is another way in which we develop our relationship with Heaven's Sherpa, the Holy Spirit—we serve. I found it so interesting that following his conversion and healing, Paul spent only a few days with the disciples before going about preaching that Jesus Christ is Lord. He immediately began serving in the teaching, missions and evangelism department, speaking as he was led by the Holy Spirit.

Acts 16:6-10 highlights how the Holy Spirit guided Paul and his companions in their missionary journeys, leading them to the region of Macedonia after prohibiting them from entering certain areas. Here was a man who was confident in the guidance of Heaven's Sherpa. Paul had cultivated such a relationship with the Holy Spirit by receiving Him, being filled by Him, obeying His lead, acting promptly, surrendering to the point of imprisonment, humility and service.

To develop a strong relationship with Heaven's Sherpa, we must be in service so that we have something to be led to. It is unfortunate how many people desire to be filled with the Holy Spirit, not so they can serve but so they can "feel" something. In some cases, it is as if we have given up the highs of the world for the highs of "feeling" the Holy Spirit. This should not be our focus. We are filled for service, we are filled to make Jesus known, and we are filled to cultivate a relationship with the Holy Spirit who will lead us into all truth. He is the One who knows what is ahead; He is the One who knows what gifts He has distributed to us and for what purpose.

Do not sit full but redundant in the body of Christ. God has gifted you for service and needs what He has deposited in you. Our days on Earth have an expiration date—refuse to squander them. Cultivate your relationship with the Heaven's Sherpa so He can lead you; and remember, when He is leading, it isn't always to a comfortable place. Look how uncomfortable it is for mountaineers climbing Mount Everest—it is dangerous. Not everyone makes it and some have to turn back. Similarly, we only have to look at the cross and the prisons where many of the Apostles ended up to see that the Christian walk isn't always about ease. I implore you to make yourself available to be led by the Holy Spirit; lives are waiting for you to step up.

Another key to cultivating a relationship with the Holy Spirit from Paul's life is the necessity and the power of worshipping and fasting. We read in Acts 13:2, *"While they were worshiping the Lord and fasting, the Holy Spirit said, 'Set apart for me Barnabas and Saul for the work to which I have called them.'"* Notice, the Scripture didn't say "prayer and fasting", but "worshipping and fasting". If you want to cultivate a relationship with the Holy Spirit, worship.

Do you know, there have been times when I have wondered what my next step would be, or how to respond to a particular situation, and then after I have begun to worship, something just shifts. It has amazed and delighted me how clarity comes, the fruit of peace manifests and I find direction for the next step. Combine that with fasting and the impact is magnified.

So, if you want to develop an intimate relationship with the Holy Spirit, worship God. Sing praises to His holy name, extol Him, magnify Him, tell Him how much you love Him; and there is no set time or way to do this. You can do this in your devotional time, while you are cooking, driving or walking—you can praise our God at any time. And remember, praise isn't just about singing songs; you can praise Him through His word, through your giving, through your obedience and more.

Take a Psalm and begin to worship God as you read it. Give God thanks for being your Shepherd (Psalm 23:1), thank Him for being your Light and Salvation (Psalm 27:1), and for being a very present help (Psalm 46:1). Praise Him for all His benefits (Psalm 103). Whatever you do, praise Him for all He has done and worship Him for who He is.

Prayer is another key to cultivating your relationship with the Holy Spirit. Earthly Sherpas recognise the significance of prayer, but we understand that Heaven's Sherpa, the Holy Spirit, is even more essential to help us to pray. Prayer was evident in the lives of believers throughout the New Testament. The Apostle Paul encourages Christians to pray in the Spirit (Ephesians 6:18), illustrating how the Holy Spirit aids and empowers us in our prayer life to communicate with God. The Holy Spirit also intercedes for us in prayer, aligning our petitions with God's perfect will (Romans 8:26-27).

Ezekiel

Many prophets in the Old Testament were led and inspired by the Holy Spirit to deliver God's word to His people. One such prophet is Ezekiel. We read in Ezekiel 11:5 that he says, "*Then the Spirit of the Lord came on me, and he told me to say: 'This is what the Lord says...'*" In Ezekiel 2:2, the Holy Spirit enabled Ezekiel to prophesy. "*The Spirit came into me as He spoke, and He set me on my feet. I listened carefully to His words.*"

As I read about the prophetic and symbolic acts that Ezekiel was led to do, I strongly believe that without faith, an unwavering trust in the Lord and the direction of Heaven's Sherpa, these could not have been accomplished. This is another key to cultivating an intimate relationship with the Holy Spirit—we must possess faith and trust in Him and where He is leading, even if it is to a wilderness, a prison or a foreign land.

Some of the actions the Holy Spirit directed Ezekiel to perform seem unconventional. At one point, he was told to lie on his left side for 390 days and on his right side for 40 days (Ezekiel 4:4-8). These actions represented the years of punishment in the northern kingdom of Israel (390 years) and the southern kingdom of Judah (40 years).

Now, I wonder how many people would have obeyed this action and, by faith and complete trust in the One who sent him, lain on one side for over a year and then on the other side for 40 days. You need to trust Heaven's Sherpa when He leads because while it will not always make sense to everyone else, as you follow, your obedience will open doors for others' salvation and redemption.

In another unusual symbolic action, Ezekiel was led to eat a scroll (Ezekiel 3:1-3; Ezekiel 2:8-10). God had given Ezekiel the scroll containing words of lamentation, mourning, and woe and instructed him to eat it. It symbolised the internalising and digesting of God's message before delivering it to the people.

When you read about what Ezekiel was called to do, it might initially seem dramatic, even far-fetched. Yet, when you see the underlying profoundness of the message God was sending to His people, the significance of these acts becomes evident. Cultivating an intimate relationship with the Holy Spirit may chart your life on roads you never expected to go, doing things you never thought you would do, yet there is no need to fear. Follow that assurance that this is the way you should go. It is borne out of trusting God and having faith that whatever He is doing and wherever He is leading, He has a plan that is always greater than our comfort, always greater than our plan or ways or thoughts.

Ezekiel shows us how cultivating an intimate relationship with the Holy Spirit will take faith and trust.

Our key takeaways

The lives of Philip, Jesus, Paul and Ezekiel give us some necessary keys to cultivating an intimate and life-changing relationship with the Holy Spirit, which include:

1. Be obedient
2. Act promptly
3. Practice humility
4. Surrender
5. Receive Him
6. Be filled by the Holy Spirit
7. Serve
8. Worship and fast
9. Pray
10. Exercise faith and trust

I believe we are called to cooperate with the Holy Spirit. To cooperate means to collaborate, unite, liaise, assist, work as a team and accommodate. We have this unique opportunity to walk in step with Him, as Galatians 5:25 says, "*Since we live by the Spirit, let us keep in step with the Spirit.*" Just as mountaineers who set out to climb Mount Everest follow their Sherpa step by step, watching where they place their feet, how they manoeuvre and even how they hold the ropes to ascend, we, too, by cultivating a relationship with the Holy Spirit, can walk in step with Him as He guides and leads.

I am reminded of the three-legged race that children and parents often participate in during school sports days. In this race, two people pair up, standing side by side with one of their legs tied together at the ankle, creating a three-legged pair. The challenge is to race in step with each other. When they first begin to run, some of the competitors often trip and fall because their steps are not in sync with those of their running partners. You will often hear them vying for leadership as they go, "Let's go, right foot first," as the other says, "No, let's do left first." One might say, "You're going too quickly," while the other shouts, "Hurry up, we're losing!" Inevitably, they lost because there was no cooperation or leadership; they didn't walk in step with each other.

In contrast, the winners are usually the ones who have paced themselves, found a rhythm and one of them tends to take the lead. The focus is on encouraging each other, "left foot, right foot", "careful, don't go too fast, we're going around a bend". So together they remain in step with each other.

That is a visual illustration of the impact of a partnership with the Holy Spirit, Heaven's Sherpa. You work together, yet, He is the One taking the lead, giving the directions, encouraging us and enabling us to walk in step with Him. I want to encourage you to let Heaven's Sherpa lead. You will hear encouragement along the way. He will let you know of the bend ahead and help you navigate it. He will teach you how to adjust to the different altitudes as you ascend in life, ministry and work. However, none of this can happen without you first intentionally cultivating an intimate relationship with Him.

12

Cultivating Your Relationship - Modern Day Examples

The Holy Spirit has been leading and empowering believers for centuries and there are numerous Biblical and modern-day examples of people that we have seen, heard of, or experienced being mightily used by God. They have all made a significant impact, whether through a first or second-hand encounter. We read about these people and hear their testimonies. You will witness examples all around if you ask God to open the eyes of your understanding that you might see Him and be led by Him afresh. The Apostle Paul prayed a prayer in Ephesians 1:17-18 (AMP), that I am praying for you as you continue your journey:

"[I always pray] that the God of our Lord Jesus Christ, the Father of glory, may grant you a spirit of wisdom and of revelation [that gives you a deep and personal and intimate insight] into the true knowledge of Him [for we know the Father through the Son]. And [I pray] that the eyes of your heart [the very center and core of your being] may be enlightened [flooded with light by the Holy Spirit], so that you will know and cherish the hope [the divine guarantee, the confident expectation] to which He has

called you, the riches of His glorious inheritance in the saints (God's people)." Amen.

Over the years, I have crossed paths with many people who have left a deep impact on me in my walk with the Holy Spirit, Heaven's Sherpa. I want to share a few examples of lessons learnt from these modern-day believers, some of whom remain a part of my life to this day. They were each able to impact me because they invested in and cultivated real, life-changing relationships with the Holy Spirit.

Pastor Veronica Joseph-Abrigo – Discerning of Gifts and Callings

Pastor Veronica Joseph-Abrigo accepted Jesus Christ as her Lord and Saviour and was baptised in March 1977. She was given every opportunity to learn by her pastor, Rev. O Parris, who taught her everything she knew about life as a Christian and the Word.

In 1983, Veronica joined the London Community Gospel Choir, a radical group of young Christians from different denominations, uniting together to spread the good news of the Kingdom of God. As people got saved through the ministry of the choir, it became apparent that they needed a place to grow in the Word and be discipled—which led to the birth of Agape Fellowship International. After attending bible college, Pastor Veronica was ordained as a minister in 1992 and took up the pastoral office within Agape Fellowship International. At first, Pastor Veronica maintained her career as a registered nurse, but after being challenged at a Mission to London event, she accepted the call to go into fulltime ministry.

Ordained an Apostle in 2003 by Bishop Bill Hamon and Sharon Stone of Christian International and Christian International Europe, Pastor Veronica has a clear mandate from God to restore true worship to the body of Christ by means of the Word, the Worship, and relevantly addressing the challenges of today's changing society through the Work.

Pastor Veronica was my first pastor. I remember frequently hearing her talk of the Lord speaking to her, and, whilst I didn't fully know it at the time, through her role modelling she was teaching me to also hear what the Lord was saying. I recall numerous occasions when Pastor Veronica asked me to pray or bring an exhortation. If the truth be told, there were times when I was so nervous I would get called to say or do something, that I would quietly get up and go to the toilet (confession is good for the soul). Yet, the Holy Spirit's gift of discerning of gifts was upon her. I remember being away at a Myles Munroe Leadership conference with her and a few others and someone telling her she was an Apostle and then telling me I was an Apostle. I had no idea what that meant at the time but, like Mary, I pondered this in my heart (Luke 2:19).

One day, Pastor Veronica asked me to pray about a particular situation for her. I was nervous because she wasn't just a pastor, but my pastor, and I didn't want to miss it or get it wrong. Nevertheless, I prayed and each time I prayed I got the same answer, "She knows what to do," or words to that effect. Hesitantly, I went to tell her and she smiled because indeed, she knew what she needed to do. I do not know if she remembers this, but those encounters, and pushing me forward to pray and share my poetry and exhortations accelerated my relationship with the Holy Spirit, because I was learning to trust, hear and obey.

Can I vent for a moment? I was nervous yet thankful and honoured in those days to be asked to serve in different ways in the house of God. For some reason, today there is a sad realisation that some followers of Christ are just looking to be fed, encouraged and prayed for with no desire to grow in ministry and service. *Lord, help us to follow where you lead, help us to desire to serve in your house with joy and deep thankfulness that you would trust us who are mere earthen vessels (2 Corinthians 4:7) to represent the Kingdom of Heaven. Selah…*

Pastor Veronica encouraged me in ministry. Even after I had left (because by now, I too was following the Holy Spirit's leading, and He had shown me in a dream where I would go next) and she was ordaining her leaders, she opened an invitation to me to join them. I thank God for the gift of the discerning of gifts and calling that operates within her life that many can attest to.

In my walk, discernment of other people's gifts and callings is something that God has sharpened and used tremendously to pull out the callings of those He leads me to, and those I am led to. That same encouragement I received from Pastor Veronica continues as people begin to walk in their God-given call.

Morris Cerullo – Boldness and Awareness of the Holy Spirit's Presence

Morris Cerullo (1931–2020) was an American Pentecostal evangelist and televangelist known for his global ministry, particularly in the area of faith healing and evangelism. His ministry emphasised the power of the Holy Spirit, faith healing, and the belief in supernatural manifestations of God's power. He conducted healing crusades, evangelistic meetings, and leadership training conferences in various countries, with a primary goal of bringing people to faith and fostering spiritual growth. He founded the Morris Cerullo World Evangelism organisation, which aimed to spread the Christian message and conduct large-scale evangelistic events around the world.

I recall going to one of Morris Cerullo's Mission to London events at Earl's Court in London as a new believer. It was one of the first times I had experienced such a tangible presence of the Holy Spirit in a room with probably thousands of other people around me. I was used to impactful praise and worship because of the musicians and worship leaders at my church, however, this felt like a whole new level.

When Morris Cerullo came on stage and was getting ready to speak, the atmosphere was captivating. He began to say, "He is here, He is here, the Spirit of the Lord is here." I didn't know what to do, I didn't know whether I should open my eyes to have a look at Him or hide. Can I keep it real? When you are a young Christian, there are so many things that are new and make sense to those who have been believers for a while, but to those just coming in, are a minefield. I tentatively decided to open my eyes to look and you know what? I didn't see the Holy Spirit! I was both relieved, because I was unsure of what I would see, and disappointed, because where was He? Right then, it was almost like I felt a comforting smile in my heart as the Holy Spirit assured me that He resides in me while also being present here in the auditorium, ready to do a work in the lives of all those present.

Those Mission to London crusades helped me to experience the Holy Spirit in a whole new way. Two things struck me about Morris Cerullo himself. The first was his boldness—he spoke with such authority and assurance, as one who had cultivated an intimate relationship with the Holy Spirit. Secondly, His ability to discern or know when Heaven's Sherpa had manifested His presence in the room inspired me. I used to leave in awe of all God did in those meetings, desiring more of Him in my life.

Pastor Doug Williams – Wisdom and Revelation

Pastor Doug Williams is the Senior Pastor of Emmanuel Community Church International, a large and thriving inner-city church in the east end of London. Pastor Doug was converted to Christ in 1978. He quickly became actively involved in children's and youth ministry for a group of local churches before going on to become the main communicator for the outstanding London gospel band, Paradise.

Pastor Doug spent over 12 years in church-planting and pastoral work in South London. He studied for a pastoral diploma at Christian Life College and earned his Bachelor's and Master's degrees at Spurgeon's College, London. Pastor Doug is a well-respected and much sought-after Christian motivational speaker and preacher with strong teaching gifts and an apostolic calling to leaders. He has a burden for the whole body of Christ and travels internationally to the USA, Africa, India and the Caribbean speaking at pastors' conferences and local church teaching seminars. Pastor Doug served for ten years with the National Assemblies of God General Superintendency team. He is also a gifted songwriter, worship leader and musician.

Pastor Doug along with Pastor Anthony were my pastors after leaving Agape Tabernacle International Ministries. Pastor Doug has undoubtedly cultivated a real and relevant relationship with the Holy Spirit. Through his song-writing and worship there is always a sense of intimacy and knowing that he isn't singing about someone he hasn't met, but about someone who he has taken time to "know".

One of the ways that I have been impacted by his relationship with Heaven's Sherpa has been through the wisdom and revelation he possesses—he just knows. I can remember being out of church more than I was in it for a season as I was ministering at other churches, events and retreats. On each occasion, I would acknowledge that he was the senior leader of the church I attended. Without fail, someone would say, "I know Doug," or "Tell Pastor Doug I send my regards," or they would begin to tell me a story of a word he had preached or how he had encouraged them. I remember saying to him one day, "Where can I go from your presence, Pastor Doug?"

I believe the reason he makes such a lasting impact on those who meet him is because he has truly cultivated a now and daily relationship with the Holy Spirit. He carries such wisdom and revelation and so when he gives counsel it comes from a treasury of what he has taken in daily and over the years. There were times I would ask to meet with him to update him on what I was doing as a form of accountability, and to seek counsel on different aspects of the journey, and he never failed to have a word in season or wisdom for the situation. Leaders near and far seek his counsel and guidance. Experiencing and seeing how the Holy Spirit operates through wisdom and revelation in his life has opened me to receive that same wisdom and revelation as the Holy Spirit leads.

You, too, can ask God for wisdom and it will be given to you liberally (James 1:5). Cultivating an intimate relationship with the Holy Spirit sharpens your hearing and your leading, so you can also walk with wisdom and revelation.

Pastor Anthony Hodgkinson – Ministry of Presence and the Father's Heart

Pastor Anthony graduated from Mattersey Hall Bible College in 1992 and began his first Pastorate in Hackney. He quickly developed a passion and gift for teaching, and especially that in regard to discipleship and spiritual formation. He joined Emmanuel Community Church International in early 2001 and was the Senior Associate Pastor until August 2023. Pastor Anthony has a lifelong passion to see the body of Christ grow in its hunger for biblical literacy and the authority of Scripture over our beliefs and behaviour.

Over the years, God has used Pastor Anthony in ways that he may never know the full impact of. I can confidently say the Holy Spirit has led him to speak words of encouragement into my life and to be present in a way that shows the Father's heart. Let me give you an example. It was while I was going through that season of "finding me" after that prayer in my bedroom when I said, "Lord make me whole, make me who you created me to be." In that season, everything in my life that could be shaken was indeed shaken. I remember feeling unsupported, looking for affirmation and approval from my leaders that I felt I wasn't getting.

Just an aside here: In my role as Senior Leader of IWC, I have learned that when some people are not yet where God needs them to be, they cannot always see the help that is being sent to them. Neither could I back then. I experienced this recently when I was checking in on one of the members who had an event coming up. When I asked how they were doing, they said they felt unsupported. I listened, prayed and then went about seeing how I could seek support for them, only to find out that about four other people had also reached out to them.

Why is this important? Because I know they genuinely felt unsupported even though support was coming from different places. What I believe happens on occasions like these is that because the support isn't in the package or presentation we want or imagine, we miss it. I believe every person in pastoral leadership at some point has had someone say something similar to "I feel unsupported". It could be, "I'm not being fed", "I feel alone," "I feel like I don't fit in" and more. Each person is on a journey and, by the grace of God, all will find what they need through discipleship and an intimate relationship cultivated with the Holy Spirit.

If that is you reading this today and you feel unsupported or like you do not fit in, I want to ask you, what is God trying to work out in you? Ask the Holy Spirit to reveal to you the times when you have been supported and the places where you have fit in, so you can give thanks. Then, from that heart of thankfulness, pray about how you can grow even closer to Heaven's Sherpa so you can know that you know that you know, you are loved, you are accepted, you belong and you are approved of. Selah...

In my season back then, God was trying to get me to see that my affirmation and approval can only come from Him. That no matter how many accolades or affirmations I could get from people, none of them match His approval and Heaven's accolades. He shared how He delights in His children, He sings over us, and He is still doing that today. Wow, what a revelation! Zephaniah 3:17 says,

The Lord your God is with you,
the Mighty Warrior who saves.
He will take great delight in you;
in his love he will no longer rebuke you,
but will rejoice over you with singing.

Returning to that season in my life, I do not know what happened, but I began to shift my focus towards God and away from what I thought I should or should not be getting. I was launching one of my books and was at peace with where I was and looking forward to it. As the book launch event was starting, I looked up and saw Pastor Anthony walking in. It touched me so deeply that I cannot even begin to articulate it. He shared some words of encouragement that day but it wasn't the words, it was his presence that impacted me.

Can I tell you? The Holy Spirit's presence does that—His presence alone can impact you so deeply that words are not even necessary.

When it was time for me to plant the International Wholeness Centre (IWC), once again, Pastor Anthony's presence over a coffee and a timely text message was indeed another stamp of his walk with the Holy Spirit spilling out in known (and maybe unknown) ways, moving me to press deeper into my relationship with the Holy Spirit.

Pastor Anthony's presence brings balance, it brings another perspective, and it impacts. Only when you have developed an intimate relationship with the Holy Spirit can you do that. I call it the "ministry of presence". There are some people who, when they show up, make you know everything is going to be alright.

Have you ever seen the joy and anticipation on a child's face at a game or sports event? They keep looking to the side-lines to check if their parent is there, cheering them on and celebrating when they score a goal or pass the finish line. That is what the ministry of presence does; it gives you a sense of security akin to a fatherly role. The Holy Spirit does that too. The Bible says "*And you also were included in Christ when you heard the message of*

truth, the gospel of your salvation. When you believed, you were
marked in him with a seal, the promised Holy Spirit." (Ephesians
1:13)

Oral Roberts – Ministry of Healing and Anointing

Oral Roberts (1918–2009) was a prominent American
Pentecostal televangelist and one who the Holy Spirit used to
heal untold lives. He left an indelible mark on the landscape
of modern Christianity as he became known for his faith and
dynamic healing crusades and televised sermons. It is believed
that Oral Roberts was a pivotal figure in the development of
the charismatic and healing movements. In 1963, he founded
Oral Roberts University in Tulsa, Oklahoma, blending Christian
faith with education. Despite some controversies, Oral Roberts'
legacy endures through his university, his influential television
ministry, and his impact on the charismatic and healing aspects
of our faith.

I had begun ministry in the late nineties with no real training
at the time, sharing poetry inspired by the Holy Spirit and
speaking at women's conferences and retreats. I knew I needed
some formal training, but I didn't know what or where to study. I
researched colleges and courses and found a programme at Oral
Roberts that fit exactly what I needed at that time. So, I enrolled
at Oral Roberts University in 2002 as an international student
and, once again, the Holy Spirit prepared me to experience Him
in a new way.

On the first day I stepped onto the campus in Oklahoma, I was so
overwhelmed by the sight of these pair of giant bronze praying
hands, that all I could do was worship and pray. I had never seen
anything like it. After registering for the course, I met a few
people. One was a doctor from a hospital nearby. He invited

me and one other student to lunch in the hospital canteen and we accepted and went to eat with him. In the hospital, there were notices about prayer meetings and he shared about praying with his patients before operations and the miraculous things that were happening. WOW! I was blown away. We had some of the best teachers in the world come to pour into us, like the late Myles Munroe, Marilyn Hickey, Ruth Graham-Lotz, Richard Roberts and others.

One afternoon, we were invited to the television studio where Oral Roberts would be speaking. He was only a few metres away from where I sat and as he spoke, he commanded the attention of all who listened. He began to call out ailments that people needed healing from and one by one people were calling in to testify that they had been healed. He was older by this time, yet his sensitivity to the Holy Spirit and his countenance screamed, "The Holy Spirit increases when I decrease", and decrease he had. We were the beneficiaries.

The anointing I felt on Oral Roberts that day didn't just emanate from within him, it was also on and around him.

As I recall this experience, I am moved... *"Holy Spirit, we don't just want You to dwell within us but also to saturate us deeply with Your Presence. Let atmospheres shift, let lives be indelibly marked as we partner and cooperate with You. An intimate relationship cultivated with You, Heaven's Sherpa, will be felt by those who come into contact with You, as we decrease and let You increase. Abba, I decrease so Your Spirit may increase in my life. I pray in Jesus' name. Amen."*

Dr Brad and Pastor Wyona Norman – Obedience, Boldness and Authority

Dr Brad and Pastor Wyona Norman were born in Durban, South Africa and raised under their spiritual parents, Dr Fred and Pastor Nellie Roberts. Since relocating to the United Kingdom in 2000, they have been instrumental in the successful establishment of several churches under the covering of Salvation for the Nations International Churches, which they established together in January 2003.

Since then, they have been sought out by many churches, church leaders and pastors who are seeking relationship and apostolic partnerships. This has led to the establishment of Reformation3 Network of Ministries & Churches, which offers ministry accreditation, as well as training and mentoring programmes seeking to restore a true biblical model for a fully functional Five-Fold Ministry in the Church today.

Dr Brad serves as Director of Faith UK TV Channel, and President of the Reformation3 College of Ministry & Leadership and the London River Bible Institute. He is a biblical academic, pastor, teacher, visionary, mentor and motivational speaker. He preaches a real and relevant word with a strong apostolic emphasis. He holds a Seminary Diploma in Divinity, a Bachelor's in Theology, a Master's in Biblical Studies and a Doctor of Ministry degree. In addition to pastoral ministry, he has served on the faculty of two theological colleges, lecturing in Systematic Theology and Pastoral Ethics.

Pastor Wyona is a sought-after preacher and conference speaker, both in the United Kingdom and throughout other nations. She holds a Bachelor of Theology degree and has completed post-graduate training in psychology and counselling. Her preaching is dynamic and prophetic. Because of the anointed impartation of present-day truth in her meetings, the deliverance ministry flows powerfully and people are set free and transformed. Healings are often manifest as God begins to deal with core issues in people's lives.

Dr Brad and Pastor Wyona are the leaders the Holy Spirit led me to sit under after leaving Emmanuel Community Church International and before leaving to plant IWC. We are still in relationship and they are two of my go-to's for counsel and accountability.

I first met them when someone who used to go to Agape recommended me as someone who could come and share poetry at one of their women's conferences. I went and shared and then was invited back over several years. I distinctly remember Dr Brad saying words to the effect of, "If that's poetry, I would love to hear you preach." Well, years later it happened, and it was under their leadership I was ordained a pastor and teacher in 2012, and released as an Apostle in 2019.

One of the things that struck me first about both Dr Brad and Pastor Wyona is the level of authority they operate in. I remember hearing them both preach and prophesy, with no apology, with no hesitation; they had heard the Lord and they were speaking what they heard. I have seen again and again how their obedience and boldness have moved their ministry forward. The Holy Spirit is a gentleman, yes, but He's not timid or apologetic. He is God all-powerful and when you meet Dr Brad and Pastor Wyona, you know without a shadow of a doubt that their relationship with the Holy Spirit is seasoned and lived out daily.

How do I know? The gifts flow freely—words of knowledge, wisdom and prophecy. Healings occur, and week by week people give their lives to the Lord as they preach the undiluted Word of God.

During the pandemic, when the world was in lockdown, they refused to shut the church doors. They stood on the Word of God and revival broke out. There is so much I have learned from this couple about cultivating a relationship with the Holy Spirit and preaching the Word, demonstrating that it stands tested above all. They continue to sharpen themselves through study and the desire to constantly serve fresh manna to the people. Their boldness in the Spirit reminds me of when Peter stood up on the day of Pentecost in Acts 2 and preached the Word of God. In verses 37-38, the Bible says, *"When the people heard this, they were cut to the heart and said to Peter and the other apostles, 'Brothers, what shall we do?' Peter replied, 'Repent and be baptised, every one of you, in the name of Jesus Christ for the forgiveness of your sins. And you will receive the gift of the Holy Spirit.'"*

What is so special about both Dr Brad and Pastor Wyona is that whilst they operate with such authority and precision in the Spirit, they are warm, generous in spirit and resources and are truly encouragers of others' gifts and talents. Many have come through their ministry and I do not believe anyone can leave their presence without being impacted for the better.

When we cultivate a relationship with the Holy Spirit, He directs us to Jesus for the forgiveness of our sins and, in turn, we receive the gift of the Holy Spirit to do the works that Jesus did, and greater (John 14:12), if we will only exercise the courage and boldness.

Cultivating a relationship with the Holy Spirit will be marked by boldness and courage to do what He is calling you to do. I know not everyone is called to preach to the nations, but that boldness can empower you to preach to your neighbours and colleagues.

I have shared just a few of the people who have impacted me in the growth of my relationship with Heaven's Sherpa over the years, but it isn't an exhaustive list. There are also many others who are spiritual sons and daughters to me, who I have seen move in step with the Spirit in such a way that I am encouraged to keep going.

I experience daily the cultivation of an intimate relationship with the Holy Spirit through my family: my mum, Normagene Peart; my sisters, Rev. Yvonne Atkinson and Marcia Peart; and my nephew, Minister Mark Atkinson. The way the Holy Spirit uses them to encourage, correct, pray, champion the call and so much more, is a joy to see. I have watched them grow in the prophetic, and in boldness and confidence in the Word and in what they believe the Lord is leading them to. When the Bible says "iron sharpens iron", this is so true of the Peart Atkinson family. In fact, the design of this book is from a direct word from both Marcia and Rev. Yvonne, as one described her vision of the front cover after we had finished praying, and the other received a dream from God. Do you not just love Heaven's Sherpa? I do!

I am honoured to have had a front row seat to some of Jacqueline Peart International Ministries (JPIM) and IWC family's growth as they cultivate their individual relationships with the Holy Spirit. From meeting many of the original members at a time when they felt they could not pray, speak, sing or preach to now sitting and being blessed week after week after week by them as they cooperate with the Holy Spirit. But God...

There is one more person who deserves absolute honour for how they have walked alongside me for over twenty-five years, even though I am unable to mention their name in this particular book due to their current mission. I could not write a book about Heaven's Sherpa the Holy Spirit without acknowledging their part. They have been guided by the Holy Spirit to speak words of life, words of caution and words of correction to me. Their obedience to the Holy Spirit could only come out of a true, tried and tested walk with Him. You know who you are and I thank God for your God-given mandate, your friendship and God's assignment for our lives.

Each example I have shared is of lives that have cultivated an intimate relationship with the Holy Spirit. Not one example is of a perfect Christian because I do not believe that exists, however, what has been evident in my journey through the Scriptures and in life is that God is never looking for perfection, but for availability and surrender.

Each leader I have sat under has given me a front row seat to different manifestations of the Spirit for which I am eternally grateful. Thank you.

13

Consequences of Neglecting a Relationship with the Holy Spirit

f we do not interact with the Holy Spirit and get a revelation of who He is, we will look to everything except to the One who can guide us, direct us and lead us into all truth. We end up where I was some twenty years ago, waiting for a leader to affirm me, when all the affirmation I needed was already inside me (1 John 4:4, Romans 8:11,16) and in the Word (John 1:1). Let's explore what the life of this type of believer looks like and the kind of problems they have the potential to attract.

We quench the Spirit

When we do not develop a relationship with Heaven's Sherpa, we inadvertently quench Him. In 1 Thessalonians 5:19, it says, *"Do not quench the Spirit."* The Greek word for quench here is *"sbennymi"*, meaning "to extinguish", "to put out" or "to go out". The word was used to refer to putting out fires, sparks, or the putting out of a lamp. Paul was exhorting believers in Thessalonica not to suppress or hinder the work of the Holy Spirit in their lives. When we do not cooperate with the Holy

Spirit or cultivate a meaningful relationship with Him, we are in danger of quenching Him.

By "quenching" the Spirit, we could end up resisting His influence or ignoring His leading.

This can happen because of two reasons: firstly, ignorance or a lack of knowledge. When we do not recognise the fire of God's Presence that burns within us as born-again, spirit-filled believers, we can hinder His impact in our lives. The Holy Spirit is a member of the Trinity and God Himself, therefore, it is impossible to put out His fire. However, He can be quenched or stifled when we resist His work in our own lives and in the Church. This is why it is so important to learn about the Holy Spirit, then learn to walk with Him, cooperate with Him and then develop a meaningful lifelong relationship, because to fulfil the call of God on your life, you need Him.

Secondly, I believe unbelief can quench the Holy Spirit. If we do not believe in His divinity and that He is co-equal and co-eternal with God the Father and God the Son, then it is difficult to believe that the same power that raised Jesus from the dead is living in us. You will think that miracles, signs and wonders are for special people or that they were only for those who lived during biblical times, instead of recognising that it is the same Holy Spirit alive on the earth today, in you and me.

If you still have any doubt whatsoever as to who the Holy Spirit is, I encourage you to go back to Section Three and read it all over again and let faith rise within you. I also challenge you to do your own Bible study on the Holy Spirit so you know that you know, that you know who He is and why He came. He is God and He wants to show you Jesus and remind you of all He said.

In the Old Testament, King Saul was chosen by God to be the first king of Israel. Initially, he experienced the empowering of the Holy Spirit and prophesied among the prophets (1 Samuel 10:6, 10). However, Saul's disobedience and lack of trust in God led to his downfall. On one occasion, he offered a sacrifice himself instead of waiting for Samuel, who was the designated priest and prophet for this work. This act of disobedience displeased God, and as a result, the Holy Spirit departed from Saul (1 Samuel 13:8-14). Later in his life, Saul continued to disregard God's instructions, leading to tragic consequences (death).

King Saul is a good example of what happens when we do not cultivate a relationship with the Holy Spirit, one that leads to us being led by Him along our journey. A few lessons we can learn from his life are:

We make it all about us

There is a spirit of pride that is rampant in and out of the body of Christ, a spirit that wants to be first, most important, receive accolades and more. It is dangerous. Saul allowed pride to enter and therefore his opinion became more important than the voice of God or God's servant. He offered a sacrifice instead of waiting for Samuel, the priest and prophet whose role it was to do so. When we fail to cultivate an intimate relationship with the Holy Spirit, we allow pride to enter—and be under no illusion, pride is dangerous. It ultimately led to King Saul's death and Satan's expulsion from Heaven (Proverbs 16:18).

We make it about people

Verses 11 and 12 in 1 Samuel 13 shares Saul's response when Samuel asks him, "'What have you done?' Saul replies, 'When I saw that the men were scattering, and that you did not come *at the set time, and that the Philistines were assembling at Mikmash [...] I felt compelled to offer the burnt offering.'"* Saul wasn't being led by the Spirit, He was being led by what he could see. He looked to please the people and stop them from leaving instead of letting the Lord build His people and His house (Psalms 127:1).

When we neglect to seek out an intimate relationship with Heaven's Sherpa, who can see what is ahead and what is around the corner, we use human intellect to no avail. We allow our emotions and people-pleasing spirit to direct us instead of looking to God.

We blame

Human beings are so interesting. Saul infers in verse 13 that it was somehow Samuel's fault because he didn't come in time. He was taking too long so Samuel left Saul no alternative but to offer the sacrifice himself. How often we blame the leader, blame the government, blame the neighbours, blame our husband or wife, or even blame the children. When we do not take time to cultivate an intimate relationship with the Holy Spirit, Heaven's Sherpa, we can become "blamers".

This isn't a new thing. It goes right back to the Garden of Eden. In Genesis 3, we read the story of the fall of man when Eve eats the fruit of the forbidden tree and Adam follows suit. When God asks Adam what he has done, instead of confessing and saying, "I messed up," he tries to blame God and in verse 12 says, *"The woman you put here with me—she gave me some fruit from the tree, and I ate it."* Did you catch that? He said, "the woman YOU put here with me", shifting the blame onto God for his error.

So, blaming others for our mistakes is a frequent outcome of the failure to cultivate an intimate relationship with the Holy Spirit.

Disobedience

It was Saul's disobedience that led him to make the sacrifice and fall from God's favour. Likewise, when we do not follow the lead of the Holy Spirit there are consequences. In my research about Sherpas, I learned that if mountaineers do not follow their direction it can lead to delays, accidents and, worse, death. The eye-opening fact about this was that it wasn't just the mountaineers who sometimes died; each year Sherpas also die due to the lack of obedience of those they are leading. Disobedience can lead to dire circumstances. Cultivating our relationship with the Holy Spirit helps us to stay in God's will and on the right path.

Saul's example serves as a reminder that even individuals who God has called and who on the surface have good intentions can falter when they do not fully trust and follow the leading of the Holy Spirit.

We regret

Saul's story doesn't explicitly mention whether he regretted any of his decisions or actions, yet I believe when we do not cultivate a relationship with the Holy Spirit, we can end up regretting not taking some of the actions He leads us to take.

I remember an encounter that happened over twenty years ago. I went to catch a bus, which is unusual because I drive to most places. At the bus stop, I met an elderly English lady who was also waiting. I kept sensing the Holy Spirit urging me to tell her, "You're one of God's favourites." I stood there debating whether that was even biblical because the Bible says, *"Then Peter began to speak: 'I now realize how true it is that God does not show favouritism'"* (Acts 10:34). How could I then say something that I could not confirm and, probably more to the point, what would she think? I went back and forth in my mind—should I? shouldn't I?—and then her bus came, she got on it and I was left at the bus stop. I cannot tell you how badly I felt. I wondered whether saying those words could have been the thing that she needed to hear, like the warden I spoke about in Section One who needed a hug. Praying for that church warden in a workplace corridor didn't make sense to me but it was everything she had prayed for and God had answered.

To this day, I use that bus stop event as a reminder whenever I hesitate to speak what I sense the Holy Spirit is prompting, because I knew I had missed a moment, something that even as I write about it now, I regret. Instead of staying in that place, however, I have developed strategies for speaking even the foolish things (in my mind but not to the Holy Spirit) so that I do not miss an opportunity. One of those strategies is that I will ask people to test what I am about to say for themselves, because I recognise that I am human and can easily miss it.

Again, I do not know if Saul experienced regret—I know I have and on more than one occasion, yet when we cultivate that meaningful and intimate relationship with Heaven's Sherpa, the Holy Spirit, we can be assured of His direction. We only need to trust Him.

Saul highlights the importance of seeking God's guidance, staying grounded in faith, and submitting to His will in all aspects of life.

I pray you will be open to cultivating a real partnership with Heaven's Sherpa and will not become stubborn, headstrong or obstinate, resisting the Holy Spirit, which is what the Bible calls stiff-necked. Acts 7:51 says, "*You stiff-necked people! Your hearts and ears are still uncircumcised. You are just like your ancestors: You always resist the Holy Spirit!*"

Conversely, there are also many examples of faithful individuals in the Bible who remained steadfast in following the Holy Spirit's guidance and reaped the blessings of their obedience, some of who I mentioned earlier.

Now that we have reached this stage in our exploration of Heaven's Sherpa, let us look at some steps to cultivating your onward journey and relationship with the Holy Spirit.

14

Steps to Cultivating Your Walk with the Holy Spirit, Heaven's Sherpa

I shared lessons from both Biblical and modern-day examples of individuals who learned to walk in step and be guided by Heaven's Sherpa, the Holy Spirit. Now, I want to share some practical steps to help you either deepen your walk or commence your journey with Heaven's Sherpa, based on some of the attributes described earlier.

Receive the Holy Spirit

Before we can begin walking with the Holy Spirit, we must receive Him by faith (Galatians 3:14; John 7:39). To receive is also referred to as the "baptism of the Holy Spirit". It takes faith to believe He is the third person of the Trinity and that He wants to teach, guide, counsel and lead you. This will mean you need to keep your heart open before the Lord with an expectant faith until you experience being baptised with the Spirit.

Wherever we turn in the Book of Acts, we find people receiving the Holy Spirit and experiencing the resulting transformational shift that comes with the experience. For example, in Acts 19:2, Paul visits Ephesus and finds that some of the disciples have not been baptised in Jesus' name; they have only known the baptism of John the Baptist. Paul recognises that these believers are missing something and in verse 2, he asks them, *"Did you receive the Holy Spirit when you believed?"*

Earlier, I spoke about being drawn, and in some cases dragged, by the Spirit to salvation because no one can come to the Father unless God draws them (John 6:44). The moment you become a believer, the Holy Spirit seals you (2 Corinthians 1:22-23) but, as Paul's question confirms, this isn't the end of the matter; there is another level in the Spirit and that is to receive or be baptised in Him.

I knew it that day in Magdalene's front room that I had received the Holy Spirit, as I began to speak in an unknown tongue, which is one of the signs. So, know that you can receive Him and you should.

So, how do you receive the baptism of the Holy Spirit? Reformation3 Bible College offers seven helpful steps as follows:

1. *Repentance from sin:* The Holy Spirit will not operate where sin holds sway (Acts 2:37, 38; 17:30).

2. *Definite experience of salvation:* A person must be in the family of God before he or she can expect the Gift from the Father (Luke 11:13; Gal. 4:6).

3. *Water Baptism (Acts 2:37-38):* However, in two cases recorded in the Bible, the outpouring of the Holy Spirit preceded water baptism. It seems Saul (Paul) was converted and then received the Holy Spirit baptism

before water baptism (Acts 9:17, 18). Also, those at the house of Cornelius believed the Word preached by Peter, were filled with the Holy Spirit and then were baptised in water (Acts 10:44-48).

4. *Deep conviction of need:* We can sometimes be unaware of what we need, however, possessing a real hunger and thirst for a particular gift and praying for it does help. God often gives gifts when they are sincerely desired and deeply appreciated (Matthew 5:6; John 7:37-39; Psalm 42:1,2).

5. *Measure of consecration:* Surrender of self-will to the Will of God. Christ makes the greatest use of the person who is willing to yield their will to God's Spirit for His direction and control.

6. *Full yieldedness of one's entire being:* So that the Holy Spirit may have His way. Often this is the most difficult condition to fulfil. After the above conditions have been met, one still has to yield his various faculties to the control of the Spirit. This perhaps is the predominant thought behind the entire Spirit-filled ministry and life.

After this, every phase of service must be the result of yielding to the power and presence of the Holy Spirit. It is impossible to tell someone else how to do this— it seems to be something each person has to learn for themself.

7. *Know that the Spirit is willing:* Seekers should know that the Spirit is willing to fill them as soon as they open their hearts, yield their lives and exercise faith. Some feel they have to tarry for the Spirit, but the Apostles didn't hold "tarrying" meetings—they held "receiving"

meetings (Acts 2). One who tarries for the Spirit believes he will receive when God is ready. One who prays for the Spirit knows He will come when the seeker is ready.

Laying on of hands

Another way we see believers receive the Holy Spirit in the Bible is through the laying on of hands. The laying on of hands throughout the New Testament is associated with the baptism of the Holy Spirit and the receiving of spiritual gifts; and blessings and curses in the Old Testament. This practice is based on several scriptures from the Bible, for example:

Acts 8:14-17 (ESV):"*Now when the apostles at Jerusalem heard that Samaria had received the word of God, they sent to them Peter and John, who came down and prayed for them that they might receive the Holy Spirit, for he had not yet fallen on any of them, but they had only been baptized in the name of the Lord Jesus. Then they laid their hands on them and they received the Holy Spirit.*"

Acts 19:5-6 (ESV): "*On hearing this, they were baptized in the name of the Lord Jesus. And when Paul had laid his hands on them, the Holy Spirit came on them, and they began speaking in tongues and prophesying.*"

1 Timothy 4:14 (ESV): "*Do not neglect the gift you have, which was given you by prophecy when the council of elders laid their hands on you.*"

2 Timothy 1:6 (ESV): "*For this reason I remind you to fan into flame the gift of God, which is in you through the laying on of my hands.*"

Hebrews 6:1-2 (ESV): *"Therefore let us leave the elementary doctrine of Christ and go on to maturity, not laying again a foundation of repentance from dead works and of faith toward God, and of instruction about washings, the laying on of hands, the resurrection of the dead, and eternal judgment."*

We see through the Scriptures shared that everyone who received the Holy Spirit did so by the laying on of hands. I remember Magdalene laying hands on me as she prayed and I received the Holy Spirit. However, this is by no means the only way.

You need faith and trust in Heaven's Sherpa

Without a shadow of a doubt, once you have received the Holy Spirit, you need to have faith and trust in Him. I shared previously how we can think we know what is next or what we are doing when it is only the Holy Spirit, Heaven's Sherpa, who knows the terrain. Only He has travelled the route you are about to take. Just because I knew the area I was driving in all those years ago after returning from that meal, didn't mean I had "omniscient" knowledge of it—I didn't realise that there had been changes in the road layout and so ended up going down a dead-end street. To be led by the Holy Spirit you need to trust Him.

So, how do you know you are hearing or following the Holy Spirit's guidance? Let me encourage you to take some time to reflect and answer the following questions to help you.

1. Does what you are hearing agree with the Word of God?

2. Do you remember a time when you truly trusted God and followed His leading?

3. How did it feel?

4. How did you know it was Him?

5. What was the outcome of you trusting Him in that situation?

6. What can you do to make this a consistent element of your walk with God?

7. Who can help keep you accountable?

8. Is there someone you can ask to mentor you as you embark on this journey?

If you can't recall a time when you truly trusted God and followed His leading, you can train yourself to recognise that better from today going forward. Start by planning dedicated time over the coming week when you can be alone, fully present and undisturbed, even if it is for just an hour.

When I say fully present, what I am talking about is not having your mind on what you will do next, what is on your calendar to attend to, or where the children are (unless you are minding them of course, and if that is the case, find a time when you can have someone sit with them so you have an hour wholly to yourself).

Then, with a pen, a journal or notepad, and your Bible, invite the Holy Spirit to reveal Himself to you through the Scriptures. Listen out for an unction to do something or a thought that lines up with the Word of God. Play some worship music and just be very present, giving attention to your thoughts and feelings and note down any Scriptures that come to mind. Also, note down any people or places that are illuminated, asking the Holy Spirit to lead you. As the faces of any people come to mind, pray for them, and as you pray ask God to reveal something about their lives that needs His touch, and to lead you if He wants you to contact them.

Can I keep it real? You may sit there and feel like nothing is happening. I want to reassure you that that's okay. Galatians 3:16-17 says, *"So I say, walk by the Spirit, and you will not gratify the desires of the flesh. For the flesh desires what is contrary to the Spirit, and the Spirit what is contrary to the flesh. They are in conflict with each other, so that you are not to do whatever you want."*

The Bible says that when we walk in the Spirit, we do not look to the flesh, because our flesh is in conflict with the Spirit. So, it does not matter if your flesh does not feel like something is happening; what matters is that you walk contrary to the desire to be in control and to feel like something is happening—simply trust, as when you do that, something shifts.

You know, I recall reading a book called *Learning the Joy of Prayer* by Larry Lea over twenty years ago, and I still remember how I felt after reading it. The book encouraged readers to spend an hour in prayer with the Lord each day, which I found exciting. As a new believer, I was ready, enthusiastic and wanted to experience the joy of prayer. So, on the first day, I set my alarm clock, got up and was ready to spend my time praying. After fervently praying about everything I could think of, I looked at the clock and saw that only about ten minutes had gone by. I was flabbergasted—only ten minutes! I was discouraged. I think I started repeating what I had already prayed as back then I lacked the wisdom to know I could pray in and with the Spirit.

Why am I sharing this? Because as you sit with the Holy Spirit, you may feel discouraged if you do not initially hear anything or sense His leading. I encourage you to persist. Know that sometimes it will be while you are in the middle of doing something different, like driving, washing the dishes or in the shower, that a revelation from your Spirit will come.

My experience has taught me not to box God in as just when you think you know how He is going to move, He will surprise you with the unexpected. Why? Because He is God. He made all Heaven and Earth and there is nothing too hard for Him. He has the world at His disposal so do not limit Him to a system or programme.

Make it a habit of giving space to hear the Holy Spirit as you start to action the things you are hearing and see what God does with your obedience. The more you do so, the more you will hear Him outside of those quiet times and intentional listening moments.

Recognise His voice and His leading

To recognise the Holy Spirit's voice and leading takes time and obedience. Whatever He is leading you to will be in alignment with His word, as the Holy Spirit will never contradict the Word of God. To help you recognise His voice, employ some of the following as you grow in your relationship:

1. *Study the Bible:* Ensure you study Scripture so you know what it says; that way, when Heaven's Sherpa speaks you will recognise that it lines up. I also encourage you to read passages that mention the Holy Spirit and meditate on them, because the Holy Spirit speaks through the Word, illuminating and highlighting truth and direction (2 Timothy 2:15).

2. *Seek Wise Counsel:* When you believe you have heard a particular direction from the Holy Spirit, it is good

practice to test it with others, like one of your leaders or someone mature and proven in their walk with the Spirit. The Bible says there is safety in many counsellors (Proverbs 11:14).

I want to add a caveat here. When you have sought advice, follow it if it bears witness within your spirit. Why do I say this? Because sometimes we are asking for agreement or approval and not for genuine input. So, we go to the first person and if what they say does not line up with what we want to hear, we go to the next one and so on. I have been there, done that and printed the t-shirt. Be open and humble enough to follow wise counsel.

3. *Pray:* Real heartfelt prayer is the foundation of any relationship with the Holy Spirit. The idea of setting aside time each day for devotion where we pray, worship, and listen to the Holy Spirit, is necessary for us to walk with Him and truly get to know Him. However, let those times be real; share your thoughts, feelings, hopes, and disappointments with the expectation that you will receive guidance, renewed hope, clarity, direction and more (Romans 8:26-27).

    In addition to praying in your native tongue, recognise that you have been given the incredible gift of praying with the Holy Spirit. He desires to reveal God's desires to us in the midst of our circumstances and relationships, and He longs to help us to pray in line with God's will. When we pray in the Spirit, we are praying along with the will of God Himself and an additional benefit while doing so is that we simultaneously build ourselves up too.

Jude 1:20-21 says, *"But you, beloved, building yourselves up in your most holy faith and praying in the Holy Spirit, keep yourselves in the love of God, waiting for the mercy of our Lord Jesus Christ that leads to eternal life."*

4. *Obedience:* When you hear something, obey and move promptly. Can I keep it real? There will be times when you miss it. There have been times when I have missed it. I believed I had heard from the Lord and moved, only to be convicted that it was a good idea and not a God idea. It will happen. Each time I have missed it, I have gone and publicly apologised or repented so that others know we can miss it, but we must still keep going. We must exercise humility and obey.

    There is a story in 2 Kings 5 that powerfully illustrates how obedience mixed with humility and faith can have a life-changing effect. Naaman was a highly respected commander in the army of the king of Aram, and he had leprosy. One of the young Israelite slave girls suggested he go to the prophet Elisha in Israel because he would be able to cure him.

    Elisha sent a messenger to Naaman instructing him to wash in the Jordan River seven times, and he would be healed. To start with, as you can imagine, Naaman was angry because Elisha didn't come to him himself and because of the instruction. He wanted Elisha to wave his hand and cure him or at the very least let him wash in one of the cleaner rivers. However, his servants encouraged him to obey, and he eventually followed the prophet's guidance. In 2 Kings 5:14, the story reveals the outcome: *"So he went down and dipped himself in the Jordan seven times, as the man of God had told him, and his flesh was restored and became clean like that of a young boy."*

Naaman nearly missed it. Yet, eventually, his act of obedience not only healed him but the experience also gave him a transformation of heart as he humbled himself. This story highlights the importance of obedience and obeying, even when God's methods seem random or challenging. When we obey, we can walk in step with Heaven's Sherpa, the Holy Spirit.

5. *Fellowship with Other Believers*: There is something powerful about fellowshipping with other believers that ignites something in you afresh. The story of Naaman also highlights how being in fellowship or proximity with others can help you enjoy a deeper relationship with the Holy Spirit. It was the Israelite slave girl that introduced him to Elisha, and it was his servants that encouraged him to swallow his pride and do as the prophet had instructed. When you do life with other believers, your life is enriched.

Another powerful gift fellowship brings is connection and confirmation. You see, there will be times when you may have thought what you were thinking or praying about was unique to you. When you gather with other believers and begin to talk and fellowship, you realise the same thing was on their hearts and minds.

This helps you to confidently recognise that the voice you were hearing wasn't your own, or the voice of the enemy, but the Holy Spirit leading and directing you. The enemy's strategy is to keep you isolated, convincing you that being alone or at home is a reasonable option, yet, when you come together with others, you realise how much you need the family of God to hear from Him (Hebrews 10:24-25, Matthew 18:20).

Practice being still

To cultivate a relationship with the Holy Spirit, we need to practice being still, which in turn helps us to become aware of His presence. When we have other things on our mind or we are distracted or busy, it is more difficult to distinguish when He is speaking or leading.

If you desire to experience what it means to have an intimate relationship with the Holy Spirit, be intentional about having quiet times where you are focused on now, not what is happening tomorrow, next month or next year.

Psalm 46:10 (AMP) instructs us to do this when it says, "*Be still and know (recognize, understand) that I am God. I will be exalted among the nations! I will be exalted in the earth.*"

Another beautiful way you can do this is by going for walks out in nature where God can speak to you through His creation. I wrote a book called *Inspirations for Seeing God in Everything* that helps people to do exactly that. Each time I saw something like a pebble or a house, I would write a poem as I was led. Ten years after that in 2017, I wrote a devotional called *Can I Keep It Real?* that shares inspirations from what I see every day—from a traffic jam to a badly parked car to a leak, revelations would just come to me. The Holy Spirit, Heaven's Sherpa, isn't restricted to your prayer time alone, He is available 24 hours a day, 7 days a week, 52 weeks of the year. Be still and experience His leading afresh.

Repentance and forgiveness

To cultivate an intimate relationship with the Holy Spirit, Heaven's Sherpa, we must examine our hearts, motives and actions daily. When we recognise or He highlights areas that need to be addressed, be quick to confess those sins and repent because God is faithful and just enough to forgive you and cleanse you of all unrighteousness (1 John 1:9).

Where necessary, seek forgiveness and begin to do what you know is right.

I feel like I need to say to someone, "GOD HAS FORGIVEN YOU!"

Oh, I need to say it louder…

Once you have confessed your sin, and from your heart turned away from what you know is wrong, know that

GOD HAS FORGIVEN YOU!

The Bible says, *"God so loved the world that He gave His only begotten son, so whoever believes in Him would not perish but have everlasting life"* (John 3:16). The reason Jesus came was for love. Again, 1 Corinthians 13:5 reminds us that "love does not hold any record of wrong".

God loves you and He holds no record of any wrong you have ever done. In fact, He also says He will have compassion on you and cast your sins into the sea of forgetfulness (Micah 7:19).

JESUS LOVES YOU…

HE DIED FOR YOU…

HE SENT HEAVEN'S SHERPA, THE HOLY SPIRIT FOR YOU...

So, whatever the enemy has been holding you prisoner with, it is time to come out of that bind. Yes, you lied; yes, you committed adultery; yes, you aborted that baby; yes, you stole that money; yes, you let pride ruin that relationship; yes, you struggle with a judgemental and critical spirit; yes, yes, yes to all the objections the enemy has thrown at you—and, yet still, though those sins be as scarlet, He will make them as white as snow (Isaiah 1:18).

Release yourself, forgive yourself and prepare for an adventure with the Holy Spirit, Heaven's Sherpa.

Remember that building a relationship with the Holy Spirit is a lifelong journey. Be patient with yourself and trust that Heaven's Sherpa will guide and empower you as you seek to draw closer to God through this relationship.

There is so much more I could have written about Heaven's Sherpa. I could have spoken about the fruit of the Spirit (Galatians 5:22-23), the gifts of the Spirit (1 Corinthians 12:4-7), the Holy Spirit in the New and Old Testament, and more. However, my assignment was to present an analogy of the Holy Spirit as Heaven's Sherpa so that He is accessible to more people. It was to help us develop a greater understanding of who He is and the role He plays in our lives in relation to an earthly Sherpa.

I pray you will engage with Him like never before. If you know Him and have been walking with Him, praise the Lord and then go higher. There are always higher heights in the realm of the Spirit.

"But you will receive power when the Holy Spirit comes on you; and you will be my witnesses in Jerusalem, and in all Judea and Samaria, and to the ends of the earth." (Acts 1:8)

"May the grace of the Lord Jesus Christ, and the love of God, and the fellowship of the Holy Spirit be with you all." (2 Corinthians 13:14)

As I conclude this Section and book, I pray the words contained within its pages will fan the flames of revival in your heart, church, community, nation and nations. I pray you have read not just for information but your heart is open for a Holy Spirit transformation.

You have read how Sherpas check the equipment in preparation for a climb—I pray you, too, have checked you have the right equipment: humility, obedience, courage, etc.—to navigate this season with Heaven's Sherpa like never before.

Before you close this book, look up the song "Oceans"[2] and, as you listen to it, meditate on the words prayerfully. Urge Heaven's Sherpa to lift you to a place of trust without borders, to lead you to walk on water, to go deeper than your feet have ever wandered, so that your faith may be made stronger. That, my brothers and sisters, is what happens when The Holy Spirit... Heaven's Sherpa leads.

---

2   Source: "Oceans (Where Feet May Fail)" by Hillsong United

Prayer of Salvation

Whether you have made a commitment to follow Christ or not, this simple prayer is for you. Try to find somewhere quiet before praying It, and then be still as you realise that the living Christ is here with you at this very moment.

Dear Lord Jesus Christ,
I admit that I have sinned and gone my own way.
I am sorry!
I've fallen into old habits, many of them bad.
I confess that there are times when I have called on you not even expecting you to answer because I felt so low about myself.
I need your forgiveness.
I am willing to turn away from all that I know is wrong, including the things that I have convinced myself are right, because I want to go with you.
I want you to be first in my life.
Thank you for dying on the cross to take away my sins.
Thank you for your gift of forgiveness, wholeness and a new life.
I now take your gift.
I ask you to come into my life by your Holy Spirit.
Come in to fill my life.
Come in as my Saviour, Counsellor and Lord forever.
I thank you, Lord Jesus.
Amen

If you have taken this step of faith for the first time, ask God to direct you to a church where you can find out more about Him and His unconditional love through Jesus Christ. Then purchase a Bible so that you can discover what God wants to say to you and about you.

Keep Climbing...

We have come to the end of our time together in this book...
but your journey with the Heaven's Sherpa does not end here.

In fact, your renewed adventure has only just begun. To
continue climbing to new heights of understanding and
connection, I invite you to visit a special section on our website
for those who want to continue to climb with the Holy Spirit,
Heaven's Sherpa.

There, you will find further resources and a community of
fellow climbers eager to share their experiences as, together,
we explore the uncharted territories of faith.

Visit www.jacquelinepeart.com

See you on the summit!

Jacqueline

Glossary

Doctrine: The word doctrine in its most literal sense means, "to teach" and/or "instruction". The original Greek word for doctrine is, *"didaskaliva"* and is defined as: "that which is taught, doctrine, teachings and precepts."

Theology: The word theology is made up of two words, *"theos"* which is Greek for "God", and "ology" which is from the Greek word logos meaning "word". Bible.org suggests the most literal definition of the word theology is, "words about God" or "the study of God".

Scriptures: Scriptures are the sacred writings contained in the Bible, given by the inspiration of God. 2 Timothy 3:16.

Word of God: The Word of God is another way in which the Bible is spoken of because it contains communication from God.

Prophet: Prophets are men and women who speak as God gives them revelation. They provide spiritual insight, encouragement, and correction through their messages from God.

Apostles: Apostles are individuals who are sent out as messengers, church planters, and overseers. They have a pioneering and foundational role in establishing new churches/ministries and spreading the Gospel message.

Selah: There are various meanings of the word Selah, however, the term is used to invite a moment of reflection, meditation, and contemplation on the words and themes that have just been shared.

Believer: A believer is an individual who has accepted Jesus Christ as their Lord and Saviour and adheres to the teachings, beliefs, and principles of Christianity, including the life, teachings, death, and resurrection of Jesus Christ taught in the Holy Bible.

Pharisee: The Pharisees in the Bible were members of a religious group or party that separated themselves from society to study and teach the Law. They were known to frequently clash with Jesus Christ over his interpretation of the Law.

Salvation: In Christianity, salvation (also called deliverance or redemption) is the "saving [of] human beings from sin and its consequences, which include death and separation from God" by Christ's death and resurrection, and the justification following this salvation.

Baptism: Baptism is the act of immersing a person in water, as a symbol of purification, regeneration, and obedience.

7 Mountains: The "7 Mountains of Influence" is a framework used to describe seven sectors of society where Christians are encouraged to have a positive impact and influence. Each "mountain" represents a different area of societal influence that Christians are encouraged to engage with, aiming to bring about positive change and uphold Christian values. The mountains are: Religion, Family, Education, Government and Politics, Media, Arts and Entertainment and Business and Economy.

References

Books:

Brother Yun, *The Heavenly Man*, Monarch Publications (2002)

Benny Hinn, *Good Morning, Holy Spirit*, Thomas Nelson (1990)

Larry Lea, *Learning the Joy of Prayer*, Kingsway Publications (1993)

Jacqueline Peart, *Can I Keep It Real? 365 Real Life Insights and Inspirations for Everyday Living*, Deep Publishing (2017)

Jacqueline Peart, *Inspirations for... series*, Deep Publishing (See individual titles.)

Online Sources:

BBC, "What does a Sherpa do on Everest?" - https://www.bbc.co.uk/newsround/27130467 9 (accessed March 2018)

CNN, "The biological secrets that make Sherpas superhuman mountaineers" - https://edition.cnn.com/2015/11/11/health/sherpas-superhuman-mountaineers/index.html (accessed August 2023)

Got Questions, "Why does God need to draw us to Salvation?" - https://www.gotquestions.org/drawn-salvation.html (accessed August 2023)

Reformation3 Bible College Course:

Reformation3 Bible College, "Certificate in Biblical Studies, Doctrine 3, The Holy Spirit"

Music:

"Oceans (Where Feet May Fail)" by Hillsong United

About the Author

Apostle Jacqueline Peart is an ordained international minister, businesswoman, author, mentor, speaker and active advocate for living and leading in wholeness. She is the founder of Jacqueline Peart International Ministries (JPIM), the home of the International Wholeness Centre (IWC), and The Wholeness Academy, which, combined, helps thousands around the globe to find and live a life of wholeness through Jesus Christ.

Apostle Jacqueline is known for her warm and dynamic preaching style, a gift that in 2009 led to her being recognised as one of the UK's leading women preachers by *Keep the Faith Magazine*, and, in 2017, one of the UK's leading black women of influence.

Apostle Jacqueline is a pioneer in women's ministry and has played a part in training thousands of women who feel a call to preach or establish ministries, through the courses delivered via the Wholeness Academy training and teaching ministry. And she is a regular guest on radio broadcasts, such as Premier Christian Radio, sharing words of wisdom and insights to listeners.

To-date, Apostle Jacqueline Peart has authored 10 books, including six in the "Inspirations for..." series; the highly successful *Can I Keep It Real? 365 Real Life Insights and Inspirations for Everyday Living*, and her latest publication, *A S.A.F.E. Place Journal...For Women*.

Over the years, as well as running her own organisations, Apostle Jacqueline has served on various leadership and oversight boards that include The Cinnamon Network Advisory Council and Reformation3 Ministries. She has also served as an Ambassador for Compassion UK children's charity.

Jacqueline is a woman of integrity and excellence. Above all, Apostle Jacqueline Peart is a woman who loves the Lord with all her heart! She is also a "family girl" at heart: despite her busy travelling and working schedule she still finds time to have fun, enjoy life, socialise and play games such as Monopoly, Scrabble and Wordscape. Apparently, she is the family's reigning Scrabble champion (though word on the street says it is actually her sister, Marcia!).

Other Books by Jacqueline Peart

Inspirations for… A Search for Wholeness

Inspirations for… Relationships

Inspirations for… Seeing God in Everything

Inspirations for… Singleness

Inspirations for… Teens

Inspirations for Women… A Journey to Wholeness

Will the Real Women of Destiny, Please Stand Up?
20 Lessons To Transform your life from Rahab

The Wholeness Equation… Living a Life that Adds Up

Can I Keep It Real? 365 Real Life Insights and
Inspirations for Everyday Living

A S.A.F.E Place Journal… for Women

Stay in Touch!

You can receive FREE weekly e-inspirations from Jacqueline direct to your email inbox every Sunday morning to help inspire you on your journey.

To sign up go to: www.jacquelinepeart.com

If this or any of the publications by Jacqueline Peart have blessed you and you want to let her know, please write to us:

Email: info@deeppublishing.com

Website: www.jacquelinepeart.com
                         www.deeppublishing.com

Follow the author on social media using #HolySpiritSherpa:

Twitter: @jacquelinepeart
Instagram: @jacquelinepeartofficial
Facebook: @JacquelinePeartoffical